# Friends in Common

## Radical Friendship and Everyday Solidarities

Laura C. Forster and Joel White

PLUTO PRESS

First published 2025 by Pluto Press
New Wing, Somerset House, Strand, London WC2R 1LA
and Pluto Press, Inc.
1930 Village Center Circle, 3-834, Las Vegas, NV 89134

www.plutobooks.com

British Library Cataloguing in Publication Data
A catalogue record for this book is available from the British Library

ISBN   978 0 7453 5058 5   Paperback
ISBN   978 0 7453 5059 2   PDF
ISBN   978 0 7453 5060 8   EPUB

This book is printed on paper suitable for recycling and made from
fully managed and sustained forest sources. Logging, pulping and
manufacturing processes are expected to conform to the environmental
standards of the country of origin.

Typeset by Stanford DTP Services, Northampton, England

Simultaneously printed in the United Kingdom and United States of
America

EU GPSR Authorised Representative
LOGOS EUROPE, 9 rue Nicolas Poussin, 17000, LA ROCHELLE, France
Email: Contact@logoseurope.eu

# Friends in Common

'I've been waiting for this book for years – a beautifully-written, compelling study of the significance of the dense bonds of friendship in fostering and preserving progressive politics. Never more needed than now, *Friends in Common* is essential reading for everyone who wants to keep hope alive; a joyful, empowering read'.

—Lynne Segal, author of *Lean on Me: A Politics of Radical Care*

'*Friends in Common* – itself the product of a friendship between its two authors – is a moving exploration of the importance and the difficulty of forging and sustaining intimate relationships within and against the capitalist hell world. Assembling an array of historical case studies, interviews, personal anecdotes and pop cultural references, Laura Forster and Joel White show that the interpersonal is political and celebrate the foundational role friendship can play in struggles for a world held in common.'

—Hannah Proctor, author of *Burnout: The Emotional Experience of Political Defeat*

'This brilliant and accessible book reveals the revolutionary potential of friendship, and how it can help to remake capitalist relations. The authors unmoor friendship from its structural constraints under capitalism, which produce isolation and alienation. Instead, they compellingly show how friendship is a method for creating political transformation at an everyday level. This book teaches us how friendship is at the core of collective ways of being together – from solidarity to comradeship – and enables these and other future modes of political belonging. An essential read for our times!'

—Miriam Ticktin, Professor of Anthropology, City University of New York Graduate Center

'A beautiful and inspiring study of friendship; *Friends in Common* is wide-ranging, original, and deeply insightful. We are in desperate need of such resources of hope.'

—Diarmaid Kelliher, author of *Making Cultures of Solidarity*

'By turns searching and playful, intimate in its project and ambitious in its scope, *Friends in Common* reframes both friendship and solidarity. A book, and, in its generosity and generativity, a gift.'

—Helen Charman, author of *Mother State: A Political History of Motherhood*

# FireWorks

Series editors:

Professor Gargi Bhattacharyya, Director of the Sarah Parker
Remond Centre, University College London

Anitra Nelson, Honorary Principal Fellow, Informal Urbanism
Research Hub (InfUr-), University of Melbourne

Also available

*Empire's Endgame:
Racism and the British State*
Gargi Bhattacharyya,
Adam Elliott-Cooper,
Sita Balani, Kerem Nisancioglu,
Kojo Koram, Dalia Gebrial,
Nadine El-Enany
and Luke de Noronha

*Abolition Revolution*
Aviah Sarah Day and
Shanice Octavia McBean

*Settler Colonialism:
An Introduction*
Sai Englert

*Practicing Social Ecology: From
Bookchin to Rojava and Beyond*
Eleanor Finley

*Reinventing the Welfare State:
Digital Platforms and
Public Policies*
Ursula Huws

*The Politics of Permaculture*
Terry Leahy

*Exploring Degrowth:
A Critical Guide*
Vincent Liegey
and Anitra Nelson

*Pandemic Solidarity:
Mutual Aid during the
Covid-19 Crisis*
Edited by Marina Sitrin
and Colectiva Sembrar

**FireWorks**

*For Denise Dowd and Evan Williams*

# Contents

Series Preface                                                          x
Acknowledgements                                                        xi

**Introduction: Why Friendship?**                                        1
  Yvonne & Jean                                                1
  letterfromjean (1)                                           5
  The Interpersonal Is Political                               8
  #friendshipgoals                                            11
  Periodising Friendship                                      16
  Friendship as Method                                        22

1  **Friends and Family**                                          29
  Good Company                                                29
  Family Abolition                                            32
  Social Reproduction                                         37
  Slippery Kinships                                           41
  Fellowships and Fraternities, Brothers and Sisters         48
  Comrades                                                    56
  *Hevaltî*                                                    64

*Conversation with Gargi Bhattacharyya*                                 68

2  **Work Friends**                                                76
  Friend First, Boss Second                                   76
  Co-conspiracy at Work                                       81
  Emotional Labour                                            89
  Wooing the Algorithm                                        96
  Gone to Brunch!                                            104

*Conversation with Gracie Mae Bradley*                   112

**3  Friends of Friends**                               117
Friendship on the Move                                  117
The Lecture Tour                                        118
Revolution Around the Breakfast Table                   121
Routes of Friendship                                    124
Friendship as the Means *and* the Message               131
Punk and Zine Circuits Through the 1990s
   and 2000s                              134
Zine Waves                                              134
Giving Up Activism                                      138

**4  Old Friends**                                      144
Encounters Across Time                                  148
Befriending the Dead                                    152
Fleeting Friendship and Anonymous
   Attachments                            158
The Anti-Family Tree                                    162

*Conversation with Luke de Noronha*                     168

**5  Bad Friends**                                      179
Spatial Tactics                                         180
Friendship, 'the Gang' and the Deportation
   Regime                                185
False Friends                                           191
Tradecraft                                              197
Patter, Paralysis                                       201
Fall Guys                                               206

**6  Friends in Common**                                211
A Band on Every Block                                   211

A Universal Language of Friendship?                     218
Friendship as a Militant Particularism               221
Friends in Common                                            227
lettertojean (1)                                                  237

*Notes*                                                             240

# Series Preface

Addressing urgent questions about how to make a just and sustainable world, the FireWorks series throws a new light on contemporary movements, crises and challenges. Each book is written to extend the popular imagination and unmake dominant framings of key issues.

Launched in 2020, the series offers guides to matters of social equity, justice and environmental sustainability. FireWorks books provide short, accessible and authoritative commentaries that illuminate underground political currents or marginalised voices, and highlight political thought and writing that exists substantially in languages other than English. Their authors seek to ignite key debates for twenty-first-century politics, economics and society.

FireWorks books do not assume specialist knowledge, but offer up-to-date and well-researched overviews for a wide range of politically-aware readers. They provide an opportunity to go deeper into a subject than is possible in current news and online media, but are still short enough to be read in a few hours.

In these fast-changing times, these books provide snappy and thought-provoking interventions on complex political issues. As times get dark, FireWorks offer a flash of light to reveal the broader social landscape and economic structures that form our political moment.

FireWorks

# Acknowledgements

This book emerges from all kinds of friendships and political movements. We hope it can nourish both. Thanks to everyone at Pluto: David Castle, the FireWorks team, our brilliant anonymous reviewers. We're really grateful to Gargi Bhattacharyya for all her support in this process and for managing to pack so much insight and wisdom into such a short interview. Similar thanks also to Luke De Noronha and Gracie Mae Bradley; we're lucky to have found such generous and careful thinkers and practitioners of friendship.

Joel wishes to thank everyone at Unity Centre, We Will Rise, the No Evictions Network and Bradford Zine Festival/ Treehouse Cafe, for transforming his understanding of friendship and solidarity in innumerable ways. Special thanks to Yvonne for the endless wisdom and to Lewis for the letter. Thanks to Toby Kelly, Janet Carsten, Lotte Buch Segal, Kath Weston, Bridget Anderson and Peter Hopkins for support in trying to write about and research all this. So many people provided insight and generative chats about friendship that informed this book, but Joel would like to offer particular thanks to: Katy White, Judy White, Steven Schofield, Joe Harvey, Merle Collett, Ailsa Darling, Rona Moffatt, Fiona Girvan, Hannah Hughes, Clara Mascaro, Billy Urqhuart, Pat Dowson, Tim Collins, Holly White, Bethan Manton-Roseblade, Mark Butterly, Reem Abu-Hayyeh, Nathanael Arnott-Davies, Jonathan

Biles, Gordon Bruce, Neske Baerwaldt, Helen Charman, Muhammad Idrish, Anna Pearce, Helen Brewer, Ludi Simpson, Tom Kemp, Lewis Normand, Ros Fraser, Lou Dear, Maria Alemao, Bridget Holtom and Luca Rutherford.

For all the above, and for taking time to read through some bits of the book in advance, thanks so much to Lilí Ní Dhomhnaill, Hannah Proctor, Maria Torres-Quevedo and Bobby Amis. Finally, eternal thanks to Laura for responding to that first email (and so many since) and to Sarah Lawson for the 'Being Alive' singalongs, and everything else.

For the many generous and instructive conversations with friends that have shaped this book, Laura would like to thank Alex Young, Joe Vann, Órla Meadhbh Murray, Al Hoyos-Twomey, Julie-Marie Strange, David Minto, Rosa Postlethwaite, Lesley Milligan, Grace Redhead, Monica Pearl, Maurice Casey, Lynne Segal, Fiona Anderson, Vic King Smith, Rona Cran, Martin Spychal, Mary Hannity, Yasmin Leung, Paul Readman, Martha Vandrei, Alice Gane, Tom Mehrtens, Nuala Shaar, Sam Knapton, Pauline Booth, Alice Roots, Melissa Wan, the historians-in-progress group in Manchester, the editorial collective at History Workshop Online, and everyone at Food & Solidarity in Newcastle. Special thanks to Željka Marošević for reading bits of early drafts and offering astute and thoughtful comments, as ever.

Peter Forster taught me so much about friendship, and I wish he was still here doing it. Thanks, too, to my mum, Julia Daykin, for her tireless optimism and support. Any insights found in the pages that follow are indebted to the friends who made me (and continue to make and re-make me). A lifetime of friendships to acknowledge, and far too many people to mention here, but you know who you are, and you make me feel unfathomably lucky. Finally, thanks to Joel for matching my relentless and unabashed enthusiasm for friendship (and for teaching me so much more!), and to Danai Katsanevaki for enduring said enthusiasm, and for making me so happy.

# Introduction: Why Friendship?

## YVONNE & JEAN

Joel is sitting in a café in Glasgow with an old friend, Yvonne.[1] They met years back through the Unity Centre, a drop-in space for people in the asylum and immigration system in Glasgow. Clear memories: the smell of the instant coffee, the sound of the printer and the old office chairs squeaking, the constant hubbub of people filling out forms, playing with kids, offering advice, catching up. Today, over tea and bowls of soup, the two of them are doing an interview.

Joel asks: 'What does friendship mean, is it a useful thing to focus on?' Yvonne thinks for a moment, takes a sip of tea:

'You know, in Yarlswood [an Immigration Detention Centre near London], I didn't know about Unity. But without fail twice a week I'd get a call from them … They would ask: "How am I? How are things?" They listened to what I had to say.

For me friendship means strength in the struggle, but vicariously. Vicarious support. If [you are inside and] two people get deported, nobody has any strength at all. But if we are outside, we are here, we are caring, you get … I don't know what to call it … like … vicarious strength?

Does that make sense? There are times when you're lying there, and you're just lost. And that support encourages you, and you encourage other people, and there is a domino effect.

Because, you know, sometimes we are coming from countries, with legacies of colonialism, capitalism, everything – that mean we can't share things, can't be ourselves. And at Unity, when these people see my file, or see my monthly report or whatever, they are seeing things about me that even my family don't know. But nobody judges nobody.

Friendship is being there for me, for people, not judging, not ... what's the word? ... taking away their autonomy – is deautonomizing a word?! (*She laughs loudly, before quickly turning back to a tone of serious reflection.*) It is two people walking together on this journey. If I laugh you laugh, if I sit and rest you sit and rest, if I'm sad we are sad together.

[It's also about not forgetting] the importance of hanging out, at people's houses, talking rubbish! To be outside all that – we chat, we laugh. It has to be natural. You have to have a love for humanity, as opposed to it becoming a cause.

This person has become part of you'.

For Yvonne, each definition of friendship necessitated another. To reframe her words is to somehow reduce the power of them, but in them we find friendship described as: acts of listening and support; an unjudgmental and intimate knowledge that contrasts with the familial; a 'love of humanity' that doesn't reduce people to an issue or 'cause';

hanging out; shared autonomy; shared personhood. Beyond the insight of each point she presents, Yvonne's words also underline friendship's shifting meaning; one short conversation on the topic produces a beguiling set of definitions, explanations and feelings. Some books about friendship would start with a similar evocation: friendship is multifaceted, hard to define, contextual. Whilst agreeing broadly with this invocation of breadth, in *this* book we are interested in writing about friendship in more specific ways, reading Yvonne's spiral of definitions not simply as an admittance of friendship's slippery ephemeralness, but as an attempt to gain some purchase.

*Friends in Common* has its roots in conversations like this one with Yvonne: trying to figure out – with friends, in acts of friendship – the links between political struggle and interpersonal belonging, and what historical resonances might help us to do so. We want, like Yvonne, to think of friendship *as* struggle, and friendship *through* struggle: friendship as both a political act in itself – a commitment to forming intimacies despite the individualising and apathy-inducing capitalist machine – and as a key sustaining force within political struggles of various kinds. We want to think about building 'vicarious strength', across difference, within legacies of 'colonialism, capitalism, everything'. We want to treat friendship as *foundational* to revolutionary projects, not peripheral to the real intellectual 'meat' of political ideas. We want to think about how friendship constitutes ideas in action, across different historical junctures. We want to understand the *life* of ideas. And to do this, we need to foreground friendship. In doing so we ended up thinking carefully about friendship's limits, what it means to build collective struggle against a capitalist system that works to co-opt, contain, and destroy relational bonds that threaten it.

Different sites can offer ways into these discussions. For Laura it was reading a John Marsden book about pen pals, *Letters from Inside* (1991), as a young teenager. In the book, one of the friends, Tracey, is incarcerated in a juvenile detention centre and the other, Mandy, struggles with abuse at home. The novel unfolds as a series of letters that oscillate between the quotidian (school, boys, pets) and earnest attempts to navigate truth and trust and ethical tribulations. For Laura the book prompted early reflection on the letter as a deliberative form of friendship, and on ideas of friendship across difference, friendship as solidarity. Years later, when living in the US as a student, these themes led Laura to the Black & Pink prison pen pal programme, and to new forms of friendship found there.

For Joel, like Yvonne, it was the Unity Centre. Opened in 2006 in Glasgow, Unity was initially focused on supporting people required to regularly 'sign' as asylum seekers at the Home Office reporting centre around the corner, but it quickly became a general hub for informal immigration casework, activism and socialising. At Joel's first Unity volunteer training session in 2016, he was immediately struck by the focus on terminology: 'We use the word friend here' said one of the 'collective members' running the session. 'Not client, or service user. Not asylum seeker or refugee. We try to say friend.' Unity made friendship a key part of its ethos and operational logic, threading together lineages of anti-racism, No Borders, Queerness and Feminism that we will unpack through this book. Later, when we started to think and write about why friendship was appearing in this way, that same collective member from Unity sent Joel an email about 'revolution and friendship' (thanks, L!). In it, they included a PDF scan of a letter purportedly written by the French novelist, playwright, poet and sometime prisoner Jean Genet. This is what it said ...

## LETTERFROMJEAN (1)

When you live with friends in intimacy, in both literal and figurative nudity, and with a real try for directness of feeling – when you have shared jobs and goals with them that help you all keep focused on the same target and moving together in a common rhythm – when the many weirdnesses and idiosyncrasies of you come floating to the surface in an everyday context (not just 'at work' or during a planned meeting), when all these different parts of oneself are explored by those around you because it affects them, because it affects the quality of our daily life, our work together, our sanity, because they must be explored, because in reality our very lives may depend on having analyzed and understood or even changed a way of behaving – when we manifest our 'love' this way (and I put 'love' between quotations because it takes so many new and unexpected forms!) and keep showing our determination to be there and to continue together – when all this happens, the densest sorts of bonds can be created. New and different ties between isolated individuals. They are born out of effort, striving. They happen. They can make you weak with wonder! A tissue of relationships that make you see many other, more official, legal, sanctioned, inherited bonds seem fragile and arbitrary. Their law holds you together in their image. After all, that's what their law is, the reflection of the power behind it.

So when I think of my experience of these kinds of rich relationships, and then I read about the history of revolutionary and resistance movements, I am puzzled. It seems that, in general, there is too much emphasis put on the roles of 'ideas', on theory, principle, ideology, as the web that holds movements together and 'explains them'. Have I misunderstood something? Does something happen in the process of writing? Is it words themselves? Of course I don't mean ideas aren't important. Perhaps they are why we get together in the first place; the light that draws us there, rather than to a religious movement or any number of other possibilities. I'm not putting down 'thinking' – do I put down apples or breathing or the sky? And especially in resistance and revolutionary movements where ideas, the life of ideas and the exercise of thought in general, has a freer and more dynamic play, a more critical role, than anywhere else within the frightened and dying society outside.

No, I am not putting it down. I am only saying that the new bonds created among combatants, the loyalties, the very new history they make together, all this goes a long way to explain a mystery: why people put up with it, how they hang together through so much, even so much 'betrayal' of the very principles they are said to motivate them. People put themselves into a meat grinder, a washing machine, a roller coaster. People try to turn themselves inside out. They go off knowing (even if only in their deepest heart) that definitions of 'success' are uncertain, ever-changing, and probably not measurable within their lifetime. For an 'idea', sure. And day to day?[2]

We've read and re-read that PDF many times since, and each time find in it something so integral to the ideas of friendship we go on to discuss throughout this book. Striving, love, combat, rhythm, the kind of 'very new history' we will go on to explain next – the resonances abound. It was this PDF that then became a key point of discussion and bonding between us, when we first started to work on what would become this book, and first started to become friends ourselves.

The story of Genet's letter is still a bit of a mystery. We can't even be totally certain that he wrote it, despite some digging. Sometimes, though, 'a tissue of relationships' can include obscure PDFs, a reaching back to claim friendship with threads of history and struggle that may otherwise have been lost. Genet's vision of mutual striving – as well as the way in which we came to inhabit his words – is foundational to this book, and to one of the orientating concepts we use throughout it: 'dense bonds'. For when Genet talks about 'the densest sorts of bonds', he captures something many of us have experienced, if not always managed to put in words. Maybe you linked arms at the squat eviction, shared a thermos at the picket line, walked that friend to a dreaded appointment, or experienced one of the innumerable other shared everyday confrontations with the 'meat grinder' of capitalism. Such interactions are animated by but also illuminate injustice, binding us in our action against it. Through 'dense bonds' we become something different, together.

## THE INTERPERSONAL IS POLITICAL

Genet also reminds us that histories of political struggle cannot be reduced to flashpoint moments of upsurge or 'capital P' politics: elections, parties, protests. He points us to affect, to the everyday, to relational ties that unsettle 'more official, legal, sanctioned, inherited bonds'. In this, he shares ground with a more well-known celebration of friendship by Michel Foucault, from an interview in 1981 in which he spoke of 'Friendship as a way of life':

> One of the concessions one makes to others is not to present homosexuality as anything but a kind of immediate pleasure, of two young men meeting in the street, seducing each other with a look, grabbing each other's asses and getting each other off in a quarter of an hour. There you have a kind of neat image of homosexuality without any possibility of generating unease, and for two reasons: it responds to a reassuring canon of beauty, and it cancels everything that can be troubling in affection, tenderness, friendship, fidelity, camaraderie, and companionship, things that our rather sanitized society can't allow a place for without fearing the formation of new alliances and the tying together of unforeseen lines of force.[3]

It is this – *the formation of new alliances and the tying together of unforeseen lines of force* – that we think speaks to the radical potential of intimacy, of friendship. This 'tying together' might happen in the street, in the bedroom, at a club, at a very ordinary PTA meeting, at the pub, at a planned political meeting, or at work. It might be formal or informal, fleeting or lifelong. These formations are radical not because they are forged by the most radical people, but because they insist on friendship as a political practice – a commitment to forming intimacies and creating spaces within which to enact them, in defiance of a capitalist regime that seeks to organise our social worlds along very different lines.

So what we're saying is that the interpersonal is political. In the twentieth century, the famous feminist dictum 'the personal is political' underscored the connections between lived experience and larger social and political structures, but it also in many instances worked as a way of avoiding intersectional critique. Black and queer feminists, notably bell hooks, critiqued white, middle-class feminists who often drew on the phrase in a way that erased their own role in the oppression of others. hooks questioned whether this type of consciousness raising was enough to build towards formations of 'a political movement which aims to transform society *as a whole*'.[4] This leap, from the liberation of one set of people to revolutionary transformation much more broadly, relies not just on an ability to politicise one's personhood, but on the web of relations that make such personhood possible: the interpersonal. Finding common cause with others means necessarily confronting difference, being attuned not just to a personal monologue of oppression, injustice and resistance but to a chorus, or more probably a cacophony, with all the messiness that implies.

This, as we will see throughout this book, can involve fleeting moments of connection or deep, dense bonds, weaved together through a lifetime. As the writers of an anonymous Zine named after Foucault's essay argue, 'friendship is political, and affinity is a more powerful foundation for revolt than identity'.[5] Playing off the classic canon of friendship philosophies – from Aristotle's typologies and ethical imperatives to Schmitt, Nietzsche, Spinoza and Derrida[6] – the writers of the *Friendship as a Form of Life* Zine join writers such as carla bergman and Nick Montgomery in asking, 'can friendship be revalued as a radical, transformative form of kinship?'[7] Cautiously, they argue, yes. While we find much inspiration in such readings, our focus in this book is less on the philosophical context of friendship and more on its everyday use, how it can both change us personally, and help us enact wider kinds of political change.

As the Zine goes on to argue, friendship can be a 'destabilizing, empowering, desubjectifying process' where 'to share a form of life is to share potentialities, to inhabit something that is possible in the future'.[8] Friendship here means an openness not just to difference, but to being reconfigured. We are formed by the structures around us, but also by the people close to us, and a central question of this book is about the degree to which we can shift our interpersonal politics into something that moves us away from cycles of capitalism, violence and oppression. As Judith Butler writes on the pain of losing a loved one: 'what grief displays … is the thrall in which our relations with others hold us, in ways that we cannot always recount or explain, in ways that often interrupt the self-conscious account of ourselves we might want to try to provide, in ways that challenge the very notion of ourselves as autonomous and in control'.[9] Yet Butler is clear that grief, like other interpersonal affects, is not a politically neutral or balanced thing: some lives are publicly grieved whilst others are dismissed. Personal loss, both of a friend and of the version of you that only they knew, brings into sharp relief the contours of a political system that values and discards life on axes such as gender, 'race' and disability.

We are constituted (and re-constituted) by the relations around us, but what we might frame here as our 'interpersonhood' is formed through lines of power and hierarchy. Understanding how this operates involves unpacking the counterproductive ways in which friendship is discussed and prescribed in our current moment.

## #FRIENDSHIPGOALS

While we celebrate and give shape to experiences of 'dense bonds' throughout this book, we don't pretend they are common for most of us in daily life. Often quite the opposite. Recent years have seen a stream of news reports about a global 'loneliness epidemic', particularly in response to the isolation of the Covid-19 pandemic. In 2022, according to the Campaign to End Loneliness, '49.63% of adults (25.99 million people) in the UK reported feeling lonely occasionally, sometimes, often or always', while '7.1% of people in Great Britain (3.83 million) experience chronic loneliness' – a sustained increase on levels prior to the pandemic.[10] Similarly, a 2023 report by the US Surgeon General's office reported that in-person time spent with friends had decreased in the US from an average of 60 minutes a day in 2003 to 20 minutes in 2020. This was even more pronounced amongst 16–25-year-olds, for whom 'in-person with friends has reduced by nearly 70% over almost two decades', with many using social media as a replacement for IRL friendship.[11] Many of these reports stress the medical risks of loneliness and isolation, suggesting sensible measures to combat this: more investment in parks and libraries, better public transportation and work leave policies, and reformed digital environments. What the 'loneliness epidemic' narrative fails to do, however, is unpack the ways in which isolation and alienation are baked into capitalist social relations. Attempts to prescribe sociality without a structural critique about this will at best be severely limited and at worst impose an exclusionary idea of 'friendship' upon a society that is denied the means to enact it. As we outline in Chapters 1 and 2, capitalism does encourage certain kinds of friendship – those that help reinforce the nuclear family unit, reproduce pliant workers, feed an exclusionary 'leisure industry', and entrench or emulate the social ties of the upper classes. Throughout the book we attempt to disentangle the way friendship has been co-opted by capitalism and deprived of its radical potential, always wary of those who advise friendship without considering how it is structurally conditioned.

Contemporary online space is one key area where friendship is co-opted and captured. While participation in online spaces can be an important way for people to connect, particularly for those in remote areas or part of marginalised groups, they are not places where cultivating 'dense bonds', in the radical sense we outline here, is much of a possibility. To argue this is not to get drawn into old debates about the 'realness' of the 'digital'.[12] Rather, it is to note the fact that social media as we know it is increasingly dominated and controlled by a small group of global corporate platforms, whose central objective is to capture and sustain our attention for as long as possible. It is widely known that many of the key tech-bros and CEOs at the helm of this industry have what many would read as anti-democratic, authoritarian and eugenicist politics, something they have embedded into the logics of their platforms. People carve out space for meaningful and important relations within these, for sure, but always while struggling against a tide of surveillance, data capture, advertising, and containment by capital.

On a more prosaic level, social media is where we engage in what we outline in Chapter 2 as 'ambient friendship'. We came to this idea through constant accidental exposure to Spotify and YouTube playlists called things like 'music to work to' or 'lo fi beats for study': streams of aggressively 'chill' wordless muzak, aimed at encouraging concentration and productivity. In an interview with the No Tags podcast, Dr Robin James articulates how such playlists reflect the people who make them – they are 'programmed for programmers, people who are knowledge workers, sitting at computers' – arguing that 'there is an economic motivation to have a frictionless and eternal stream': keeping you online.[13] We can apply a similar logic to the social media apps that structure our most intimate everyday interactions. These platforms mirror the ideologies of their creators: friends should be accumulated and networked, sociality is monetisable, virality and conflict drive traffic. Friendship in such environments feels busy. There is no shortage of connectivity, because connectivity keeps us online, increasing advertising revenue and opportunities for data gathering. Actual connection is harder to find though, with many of us exhausted by the constant pressure of unread and unresponded-to messages: friendship starts to feel like networking, in platforms designed by people who see little difference between the two.

Online space is also where many of us encounter prescriptive ideas about friendship: 'ditch those toxic friends', 'you are the average of the people you surround yourself with', 'best friends are the best therapy', #friendshipgoals. These overlap with and are reinforced by a far wider set of cultural forms: TV shows, books and films extol narrow ideas of 'the squad', 'the bromance' and the 'BFF', while 'Friendship Networking Apps' tell people, 'If you haven't found your tribe yet, don't panic – there's your whole life ahead of you with Bumble For Friends.'[14] A fast-growing industry of friendship coaches, podcasts, manuals and self-help books speak to a real widespread desire for improved relations but fail to name the structural limits underlying this. Instead they focus on individualised prescriptions: 'change your mindset', build 'frientimacy', recover from being a 'friendaholic'.[15] Such prescriptions imply a set of assumptions about friendship: that it involves transaction and instrumentality between bounded individuals, 'nice' sentiments (with occasional surmountable fall outs), shared social status and a tiered hierarchy, with 'best friends' sitting slightly below romantic partners (a friction deliberately evoked when married couples talk of having found their 'best friend'). In writing this book we've come across an overlapping set of questions: How does friendship deal with difference? Do we have to get along to organise politically? Do we have to enjoy it? Doesn't friendship imply cliques, social exclusions, tiers of belonging? We find such questions productive, but essentially rooted in the same thin, limited visions of friendship we are offered under contemporary capitalism. As Yvonne and Jean show us, and as we go on to demonstrate throughout this book, friendship can work across and with difference, beyond the limits of 'nice' sentiments or existing social groupings.

As we outline in Chapter 2, dismissive caricatures of friendship often coincide with defences of 'the comrade', depicted as a more serious and effective form of political belonging, tied to the party form. These sometimes construct a vision of 'real' political work as definitionally sombre and disciplined, missing not only the messy affective realities of even the most officially 'comradely' groups, but also the potential for new forms of friendship and comradeship to emerge in dialogue. Relatedly, while other advocates of friendship may focus on the 'pleasure' and 'joy' it can generate in struggle, we are wary of this becoming a two-dimensional counterpoint to the projected image of the true activist as pointedly ascetic and stoic.[16] Political struggle should not be defined by how miserable or joyous it is, and joy is not the only affect. As Hannah Proctor, drawing on the writing of Kate Millet and Luisa Passerini, argues, political belonging is also shaped by defeat and despair, including 'the solidarity of disappointment'.[17] Friendship, when we try to unmoor it from capitalist social relations (and especially when we try to confront these), is not always happy or comfortable. It is important not because it is 'nice', but because it is where we learn, work through, and reimagine the social fabric of our lives.

This book does not offer diktats or guidelines for friendship. We do not presume to know exactly what friendship might look like for different people, in different times and places. In the course of writing the book, people have sometimes asked us whether we are dismissing the enjoyment of solitude, or ignoring the experiences of introverted and neurodivergent people. Such questions reimpose the kind of normative ideas of friendship we outlined earlier, rather than allowing us to consider the political structures that inform how we organise social life. They presume that certain people are already somehow less 'social' than others, rather than being open to the multiple forms that sociality can take, and unpacking how these are produced. All of us are woven together in some way, and personal desires for friendship (its scale, form, time in life) can change over time. These desires are informed not just by cultural scripts and personal feelings, but by deeper material and historical shifts, which we now overview.

## PERIODISING FRIENDSHIP

It is our contention that friendship has, over the last 40 years, taken on a particular salience in how people enter left-wing political struggle and conceptualise their political belonging. For much of our lifetimes, it has been a kind of unspoken common sense. People might join political parties or get active in different campaigns, but – for a considerable majority and over the long durée – their political lives happen with and through friends. A range of contemporary political spaces and activist repertoires, from the public square to the protest camp, have threaded notions of affinity and friendship within their varied iterations during this period. Though not always focused explicitly on friendship, different writers have attempted to frame this shift in various terms: as a reaction to the end of the Cold War and the failures or violent suppression of various communist projects; as an encroachment of neoliberal subjectivity; as an attempt to evade police tactics that target formal political structures; or as a generational rejection of 'old' hierarchical tactics.

Vincent Bevins, in a sweeping account of the 2010s 'protest decade', exemplifies such analyses in charting a historical shift from the New Left of the 1960s and '70s to the 'alter globalisation movement' of the 1990s–2000s. Where New Left interventions 'insisted that means also mattered in addition to the ends', Bevins argues that this changed throughout the 1980s and 1990s to a position where 'the means were the ends': where horizontalist organising models, autonomous zones and the interpersonal relations formed within both took precedence over vanguards or cadres aimed at seizing state power.[18] Organising for a revolutionary rupture was supplanted by a focus on direct democracy and direct action in the here and now, on forms of democratic organisation that were often inspired (sometimes in extractive ways) by Indigenous and non-Western practices. Prefiguration, the idea of embedding our dreams of future political config-urations in contemporary practice, takes on increasing prominence in such a narrative – with an attendant focus on interpersonal ethics, accountability and spontaneity, and a rejection of political representation. The artist and campaigner Tori Abernathy offers a typical summary of how such activists connected friendship and political struggle: 'Friendship has been and always will be the basis of political action. The point of prefiguration is bringing the future into the present and the primary way that we do this is in the forming and nurturing of our relationships with one another in the ways we enact them on a day-to-day basis.'[19]

Bevins, drawing on prominent anarchist writers such as David Graeber, maps these shifts onto the ascendance of anarchistic organising models during the period. High profile anarchist collectives such as CrimethInc explic-itly centred friendship in their writing,[20] alongside many other proponents of 'affinity groups' as an ideal unit for bringing 'activists together on the basis of friendship in small, fluid autonomous groups to ferment revolution in the wider population.'[21] Bevins argues that these ten-dencies operated with a certain (often unconscious) notion of historical progress: 'many people in my gen-eration (and I think I, too, was guilty of this teleological mode of thought at the beginning of the decade) thought that if you simply gave the thing a kick, it would come unstuck and move in the right direction.'[22] This suggests a contrast with earlier 'stagist' or deterministic ideas of historical change, whereby much anarchist *and* communist theory from the early twentieth century assumed that an inevitable, evolutionary shift away from capitalism was imminent. Friendship's appeal as a mode of political belonging and political imagination increases where more totalising accounts of capitalism's end lose their explanatory purchase. Rather than reading it simply in terms of a lack or absence (of 'real' political organisation), friendship should be seen here as an important, historically contingent social phenomena that deserves serious analysis.

Our periodisation of this form of friendship draws on the communist theorising of the Endnotes Collective.[23] Though we doubt the group would share many of the arguments about friendship presented in this book, their historical analyses are very useful for considering how forms of left-wing political belonging orientated to the 'workers movement' have collapsed in the last 50 years. Endnotes argue that the 1970s constitutes a 'periodising break' whereby huge changes in labour process, the decline of a global peasantry, a slowdown of capitalist accumulation, continued overproduction and rampant deindustrialisation fundamentally reconfigured the material (and relational) context in which worker organising could happen. Despite this, much communist and socialist theory and practice continued to focus on a narrow vision of the 'collective worker': a kind of universalising avatar of the industrial labourer that would drive the inevitable wheels of history through capitalism and into a bright new future.

As Endnotes argue, this was from its inception a mythic figure: 'the collective worker – the class in-and-for-itself, the class as unified and knowing its unity, born within the space of the factory', to a large extent 'did not exist outside of the movement's attempts to construct it'.[24] Historic and emerging differences within the working class, often deliberately drawn upon in capitalist attempts to divide and control it, were in constant tension with the assumed unification of this class. Instead of increasing unity and solidarity, Endnotes argue, what these shifts ultimately created was 'unity-in-separation', as 'people become ever more interdependent through the market, but this power comes at the expense of their capacities for collective action'.[25] Here, the alienating dynamics of the division of labour and capital's marketisation of our social relations predominates over forms of social solidarity, which, in a world of collective atomisation, become harder to imagine and harder to organise from within. To move beyond this requires detailed analysis of contemporary capitalism, but also ideas for building collective power against 'unity-in-separation', 'without appeal to a pre-existing metaphysical entity, the collective worker'.[26] We suggest that friendship is one important entry point into such a project, not as a replacement for the 'collective worker', but as a space for practising and imagining future modes of political belonging, informed by radical histories and engaged with existing forms of contemporary sociality. As we will go on to argue in Chapter 2, the role of friendship within the workers' movement, and in the residual threads of this today, offers a less nostalgic way to take up the struggle, and to uncynically analyse the drift away from formal comradeship.

Charting this shift in a more encompassing way than we've just sketched is beyond the scope of this book.

Instead we offer a multiplicity of historical examples, using the words and actions of people who have built friendship into struggle. We draw predominately from Europe and North America. This is clearly a limitation, and while in our final chapter we talk extensively about global solidarity and problematising the global/local binary, we wanted to write predominately about the political context within which we've organised, in the hope that this will resonate and offer a way in for others to do the same in different contexts. Our historical limits are also deliberate. We mark the post-1970s shift sketched above (culminating in the 1990s–2000s organising methods we inherited) and the end of the nineteenth century (c.1880–1914) as two key eras when friendship was ascendent in political organising in Europe and the US – though this tendency has always reached out to other international struggles and sites, and never been completely bounded. Our focus on the nineteenth century is in part because Laura's historical research has centred on the radical movements of the Victorian era, and this has therefore shaped her own political consciousness. It is also because the acceleration of modern capitalism in that century prompted by its end a range of vibrant experimental movements – including early environmental, animal rights and homophile groups – and a whole swathe of anarcho-socialist tendencies that practised and preached friendship in radical ways. Throughout this time, people found ways of inculcating 'dense bonds', communicating across emerging internationalist movements, using new technologies and transport infrastructures, and finding friends in common. All of this provides important context for understanding how sociality and friendship can (and could!) figure in struggle today.

## FRIENDSHIP AS METHOD

Histories of friendship, and the sustenance such histories can offer, also help us to understand friendship as method. Excavating friendships is a means through which to recover some of the more diffuse ways in which political ideas are generated, appropriated and propagated. Finding friendships in the past can help to challenge big narratives that don't always make space for the nuances of intimate human connection, or for the affective nature of political engagement. The privileging of certain source materials – political pamphlets, organisation and union records and minutes, and political speeches – within histories of the labour movement often skews analysis away from themes and characters that are less well represented in easily reached archival material. But political sentiments are very often expressed and developed through friendships, fleeting discussions and intimate, informal communications. The search for these friendships and expressions of intimacy, therefore, is an attempt to reconstruct the more elusive emotional worlds of activists of the past.

In looking to the anarcho-socialist experimenters of the late nineteenth century, as we do throughout this book, we find friendship is an important means of historical recovery. The fact that these movements were animated by relationality and informality means that the historian seeking to trace the genealogy of these radical ideas via organisational records alone would struggle, or else might declare them unsuccessful or of little consequence. For many of these people their institutional affiliations were fluid. Most were members of several overlapping, precarious and short-lived organisations, and they contributed to various publications and projects. Much of their 'doctrine' was not elaborated at conferences or through an understanding of orthodoxy; they did not have political parties proper, and they rarely had binding official documents. Their frameworks for creating and disseminating political ideas were often fluid and informal. This was a living movement, one animated through friendships, conversations over beers and books, encounters on street corners, in friends' living rooms and in crowded meeting rooms. This was the everyday life of social movements. For the historian, therefore, the social history of these ideas is fundamental to understanding the ideas themselves. Only by looking to all manner of connections, coincidences and more diffuse records can we hope to recover the intellectual currents that animated these forms of struggle.

In this, we draw on the tradition of 'history from below', outlined by key practitioner Marcus Rediker as a mode of history 'that concentrates not on the traditional subjects of history, not the kings and the presidents and the philosophers, but on ordinary working people, not simply for what they experienced in the past but for their ability to shape the way history happens'.[27] Emerging from the New Left moment, the 'history from below' approach did much to strengthen and inform the struggles of that era, as part of an interplay between social movement history and activism that has arguably waned in more recent years. We hope this book can contribute to recent renewals of the interconnection between history and struggle,[28] overlaying examples from past and present in order to illuminate commonalities and possibilities that may have been suppressed by traditional historicisation. This is a process we tentatively began thinking of as 'history from within': within the present, within the struggle, within our relationships. Here, we also find much insight and inspiration in the work of Black feminist writers such as Saidiya Hartman and Shola Von Reinhold, who engage history through speculative fiction (what Hartman calls 'critical fabulation') to reimagine lives that have been elided or silenced by the archive.[29] Though clearly different from our more empirical focus, we find in such work a reaching out past the codified and historicised walls of state, nation and traditional history. Here, we are also inspired by queer invocations to 'remake the past to reimagine a new temporality',[30] where what the writer Nicole Wolf calls 'speculative friendships' can assist us in acts of 'looking back to project forward'.[31] Ideas of past, present and future structure our lives in deeply entangled ways, as Lola Olufemi writes in *Experiments in Imagining Otherwise*:

> My aim is to produce a map that is nothing like a map at all but rather a record of traces that make connections between the past(present/future) – the present(future/past) – and the future(past/present). I want to demonstrate how these temporal regimes encroach on one another, so to tell the story of the past means telling the story of the present, which is already where the future resides.[32]

We hope this book helps conjure such maps in some way too, unsettling not just capitalist and colonial temporality, but also the ways that these systems produce ideas of peoples and space divided into immemorial, essentialised units. Using friendship as an organising method through which to bring together varied and rich histories punctures such fictions.

Friendships themselves are archives of all the informal, intimate and irreplicable affects and ideas that can create revolutionary subjectivities. These scrambled and diffuse archives remind us that friendships and everyday solidarities do not simply provide a means through which ideas can spread and cohere, but can also in themselves generate ideas and identities. These histories of friendship are fundamental to our understandings of struggle. David Featherstone emphasises 'the importance of mobilising usable pasts in ways which are attentive to the geographies of connection that made up past struggles'.[33] In this way, excavating friendships of the past is a vital means of recovering connections, multiplicities and mobilities that were central to some of the forms of struggle explored in this book. Recovering and writing histories of friendship is a way of multiplying these connections, of making real, small and embodied solidarities echo louder down the years. These friendships are not universal, they cannot be scaled or abstracted to fit all, but they can reverberate and multiply, and in doing so they *can* reach out across time and space.

To summarise then, *Friends in Common* builds a number of related arguments about friendship. Firstly, that the interpersonal is political: the way friendship operates in contemporary life is conditioned by power and hierarchy, but there is radical potential in reconfiguring our bonds of intimacy. Secondly, and relatedly, that capitalism co-opts and conditions friendship in profound ways, but these are never complete, and that looking to the multiple and often radical forms friendship takes at different times – without resorting to prescriptive diktats of our own – can help us challenge the capitalist system. Thirdly, that friendship as a specific mode of radical political belonging ascends at different historical junctures – in our analysis, in the late nineteenth century and post-1970s. Through the book we hope also to show friendship as a kind of bridging concept allowing for a productive traffic between differ-ent scales and binaries: personal-political, private-public, local-global.

In Chapter 1, we situate friendship within debates around family abolition, arguing that it is a useful, exist-ing set of practices for practically moving away from the imposition of nuclear familial units. In Chapter 2, we consider how friendship and work overlap, drawing out struggles within and against work, around leisure and emotional labour, and in online life. Chapter 3 focuses on how friendship is made tangible and put in motion, looking at travelling activists in the nineteenth century and the 2000s Punk Zine Circuit. Chapter 4 considers the potential of intergenerational friendship, also con-sidering grief, encounters across time, and the Kurdish idea of *hevaltî*. Chapter 5 looks at 'bad friends', how the state polices friendship through the control of space and the social infiltration of radical movements. In our final chapter we consider the potential, and pitfalls, of friendship as a way into solidarity, showing the interconnection of 'local' and 'global' struggles.

*Friends in Common* draws on examples from pop culture – Stephen Sondheim musicals, 1980s and 2000s punk, high and low brow TV – along with history, literature, anthropology, anecdotes, letters, and much more. Alongside these, we have included three short 'conversations' with people who were important to this project: Gargi Bhattacharya, Gracie Mae Bradley and Luke De Noronha. These interviews help us connect and introduce the various threads of the book: how friendship intersects with history, family, work, movement, intergenerational connection, the state, and wider forms of solidarity. Through these various sources we wanted to give a maximalist sense of friendship as a conversation and a process, and as something that is present in all kinds of contemporary practices and mediums. Our examples reflect the periodisation we've just outlined, along with the particular focus on friendship we find in our current moment – a moment defined by the lingering afterlife of a global pandemic and the ongoing 'polycrises' of climate catastrophe, far-right resurgence, precarity, economic hardship, rising anti-LGBTQ politics, spiralling conflicts around the world, and Israel's continuing genocidal decimation of Palestine. Responding to the overwhelming scale of these intersecting crises can feel impossible, but building upon established practices of interpersonal connection and imagining new forms of political belonging are vital in moving beyond isolation and inertia.

Throughout the book, we return to friendship as a range of existing practices, something tangible and already in motion, something that matters to people. As Yvonne made clear at the start of this intro, 'vicarious strength' requires acts of friendship, never reducible to theory alone.

'For an "idea", sure. And day to day?'

# CHAPTER ONE

# *Friends and Family*

## GOOD COMPANY

*Someone to crowd you with love*
*Someone to force you to care*
*Someone to make you come through*
*Who'll always be there*
*As frightened as you*
*To help us survive*
*Being alive.*[1]

So ends 'Being Alive', the centre-point ballad of Stephen Sondheim's musical *Company*. Originally performed in 1970, the show deals with themes of dating, marriage, love and loneliness as it follows a self-involved bachelor called Bobby on his thirty-fifth birthday, surveying his life in a state of near-dissociation, through eleven vignettes featuring his various married friends.

The title of the musical reflects the role Bobby plays for these friends, or at least how he perceives this. Bobby drifts around the domestic lives of his friends at various parties and nights out: 'company for dinner', company to adjudicate arguments, company to witness the vagaries of unhappy marriages, company to remind them that loneliness is worse. Bobby acts as both a sounding board and an imaginative limit for his coupled companions, who

constantly berate him for not 'settling down' whilst simultaneously bemoaning their own difficult relationships.

Sondheim wrote in his lyrical memoir, *Finishing the Hat*, that the musical is about the 'challenge of maintain-
ing relationships in a society that is becoming increasingly depersonalized',[2] which is maybe why it hit so hard when Joel first watched it, at the height of the Covid-19 lock-
down, as part of a weekly online viewing party organised by a friend. (Of course, being on a Monday, it became called 'Mondheim'.) Despite these themes, *Company* is often read as a celebration of marriage, as the centre point of the familial unit, 'warts and all'. This seems odd, considering the veins of acerbic scepticism and satire that run throughout the musical. Despite Bobby's hetero-
sexuality, the musical's questioning of the appeal of the monogamous family unit feels decidedly queer and crit-
ical – reflecting Sondheim's own positionality (though he reportedly hated such interpretations), and pre-empting debates around the liberatory potential (or not) of gay marriage. A 2021 revival of the musical lent into such themes, flipping Bobby's gender (now 'Bobbie', in a familiar depiction of the 'ageing' single woman) and including a gay couple on the verge of marriage.

'Being Alive', the song where Bobby/Bobbie comes to terms with the beginnings of desire for longer term love and emotional commitment, was originally written by Sondheim as 'Happily Ever After', in a less sympathetic mode. Producer George Zadan recounts director Harold Prince calling this early version 'the bitterest, most unhappy song ever written, and we didn't know how dev-
astating it would be until we saw it in front of an audience.

It scared them and it scared us because it was too complicated … If I heard that song I wouldn't get married for anything in the whole world.'[3] This context helps us appreciate the song's ambivalent message, reflecting not only Bobby's growing sense of wanting to shed his notions of self-sufficiency and self-containment, but his realisation that societal norms restrict him to narrow, nuclear familial containers for this. 'Being Alive' encapsulates Bobby's growing sense of the impossibility of finding emotional connection and care outside of marriage and the nuclear family, along with the relationship between care and coercion: '*Someone to force you to care*'.

As such, *Company* offers a rare depiction of how friendship is often instrumentalised towards the maintenance of marriage and nuclear family units. This, despite friendship being depicted as naive, childish, or sometimes an anathema to such structures: our dominant cultural and societal scripts only encourage certain kinds of friendship, the kinds of 'good' company that facilitate 'good' families.

As *Company* underlines, it's hard to think about friendship without thinking about family. The two ideas exist in symbiotic relation to each other, sometimes directly opposed, sometimes overlapping. In this chapter we outline the ways in which friends and family are interconnected, arguing that friendship can play an important role in moving beyond the way normative nuclear families structure and reproduce capitalism. We ask how friendships and interpersonal connections help sustain such systems, beginning by outlining theories of family abolition, and what an analysis of friendship might contribute. We then unpack how both family and friendship feature in social reproduction, the ways in which care is organised to sustain and produce workers for capitalism, or what Emma Dowling calls 'the work of producing labour power and life'.[4] In the second half of the chapter we consider how slippages between kinship terms can be productive, exposing the socially contingent meanings of apparently solid ideas like 'family' and 'biology'. We finish by looking to different terms of political belonging that have historically combined (or rejected) family and friendship: fellowship, fraternity, comradeship and Kurdish *hevaltî*.

We all need people to 'help us survive, being alive', but how do we name these forms of intimate political belonging?

## FAMILY ABOLITION

The project of family abolition is central to our understanding of friendship. Theories of family abolition offer a critique of the role that the white, heteronormative nuclear family plays in reproducing capitalism, whilst also considering other forms of social being: the commune, the comrade, the unknown post-revolutionary relation. M.E. O'Brien sketches a history of recent theorising on the topic that includes her friend Sophie Lewis's writing, along with scholars such as J.J. Gleeson and K.D. Griffiths, Kathi Weeks and Tiffany Lethabo King. As she argues, 'the family is a limit to human emancipation ... a joy for some, a necessity for most, and a nightmare for too many'.[5] Nuclear families lock people into models of property (husbands own wives, parents own children), scarcity (care is contingent on finding and maintaining familial ties) and invisibilisation (hiding violence and abuse 'behind closed doors', masking the unpaid labour necessary to sustain everything). It is no accident the heteronormative family is so central to right-wing politics, structuring myths of government as a 'household', and of a racialised 'national family'. On a deeper level, the family is both the foundational economic cell of capital and the domain where its alienated logics become embodied and internalised. O'Brien shows how, in our system of wage labour and meagre state support, families are integral to survival for most of us, and the difficulty of both reimagining and materially moving past the family is part of the reason it is necessary to do so.

Family abolitionists like Sophie Lewis think particularly carefully about how their critiques come up against the ways in which familial care has been central to Black liberation struggles, Indigenous life and migrant solidarity. Lewis advances a 'critically utopianist position' that shows how family abolition has been central within these liberation traditions, rather than imposed from outside them. For instance, Tiffany Lethabo King has paid particular attention to how contemporary ideas of the family emerge from legacies of slavery and anti-Blackness. King draws on a rich history of Black feminist critiques of the family that reckon with the enforced 'kinlessness' of slavery and subsequent state violence against Black families, arguing that 'critical and innovative world-making traditions of Black life must envision life outside of the current categories' of familial relation.[6]

The historical advent of the white bourgeois family was concurrent with violent erasure of other forms of kinship.

O'Brien demonstrates how 'racial capitalism took shape in North America through consolidating a white family of property and through relentless attack on Indigenous and Black kinship relations'.[7] In opposition to such processes, family abolitionists draw attention to the potential of anti-capitalist and communist forms of relationality. Scholars of prison abolition have long focused on the creative potential of abolition, a 'presence', in Ruth Wilson Gilmore's terms,[8] that gestures not simply to the absence or destruction of state infrastructures, but to the nurturing of forms of care that could take us beyond the violence of our current system. Similarly, family abolition entails rethinking how our social fabric might be reconstituted. In O'Brien's words: 'Family abolition is the care we all need abundantly available beyond the family. This care could extend through the whole of society, made possible through deep revolutionary change. Family abolition is the expansion and generalization of relations of care and consensual interdependency.'[9]

Friendship rarely features in this body of work. Lewis and O'Brien are more interested in the way abolition offers a 'horizon' for thinking through new forms of sociality, 'a way of theorizing a postrevolutionary free society' in O'Brien's words.[10] We depart slightly from O'Brien here in terms of the degree to which we read capitalism as a totalising system, conditioning every aspect of social life. Theories of family abolition offer profound tools for reimagining how care and relationality could be organised, but we argue that friendship – as both an existing, meaningful set of practices and ideas that people are committed to day-to-day, and a space where possibilities for other forms of social life can be experimented with – can help illuminate the forms of life not totally captured by capitalism. For us, it is *within and through* such practices that new and unknown forms of anti-capitalist sociality can be imagined and struggled towards.

Throughout her work, O'Brien paints a vivid picture of moments of 'insurgent social reproduction', when spaces like protest kitchens, pickets and barricades become sites of new, liberatory social formation. We also see this possibility in far more everyday sites of friendship, and in the connections between the two. Here, the primacy of the normative family is chipped away at in small but profound ways, from the friend who helps someone get out of an abusive domestic situation, to the ad-hoc childcare rota or the whip-round for a friend's rent. Friends are often the first port of call when family fails, as it so often does. They are also the way many of us find other forms of support, leading us to political groups, campaigns, community spaces and new forms of collectivity. Friendship can be a site of everyday family abolition, of prefiguring new possibilities for social organisation. It is a bridging concept – from the personal to the interpersonal, from identity to affinity – that lets people taste the possibilities of interconnection and solidarity at different scales, gesturing towards radical forms of sociality in the future.

Friendship is not easily codified or contained. As Sophie K. Rosa argues, 'the unwieldiness of friendship – understood as polyvalent intimacy that defies hierarchy, formalisation and state sanction – could be its power'.[11] Ultimately it is this unwieldiness that makes friendship a threat to normative ideas of the family. Rosa offers this argument as part of an analysis of the finale of the TV series *Friends*, essentially a 'wake for friendship',[12] where the main characters are all parcelled off into nuclear, heteronormative futures (apart from Joey, the eternal buffoon-bachelor, who gets his own spin-off series). In such cultural scripts, friendship largely ends where family begins, a youthfully naive prequel to a 'real life' of wage labour, property ownership and family rearing. Unsurprisingly, considering capitalism's reliance on the nuclear family form as what Mario Mieli calls 'the cell of the social tissue',[13] 'friendship is ascribed less value than romantic and sexual relationships, the onset of which often signals the beginning of the end, or at least significant dilution, of platonic bonds'.[14]

In much left-wing thinking around friendship similar assumptions crop up. Friendship is depicted as an adjacent, unserious part of activist and revolutionary life, sometimes placed chronologically alongside 'baby queers' and 'baby anarchism', before 'real politics' and disciplined collective action take hold. We want to push back against such assumptions here, whilst being attentive to the genuine difficulties many people face in maintaining active friendships in the face of ageing, increased work loads, childcare and elderly care. We see friendship as a tool both for collectivising care day-to-day and for addressing the imposed scarcity of care under racial capitalism. To really explore these possibilities, we also need to think carefully about the family-friendship binary, and how it masks the ways in which friendship is also folded into the reproductive circuits that sustain capitalism.

## SOCIAL REPRODUCTION

As we highlighted at the start of this chapter, part of *Company's* power is that, in scornfully capturing the limits of a certain kind of upper-class sociality (opera, extravagant lunches, refundable birthday presents), it gestures towards the possibility of a different kind of interpersonal connection. It's easy to be cynical about the often numbed and instrumental kinds of 'friending' we see in online social media and dominant media: 'a banal affair of private preferences: we hang out, we share hobbies, we make small talk. We become friends with those who are already like us, and we keep each other comfortable, rather than becoming different and more capable together.'[15] Yet such relationships point to a deeper desire for connection, and to the ways in which, despite the central atomisation of capitalist social relations, certain kinds of elite sociality and leisure are encouraged. Theories of social reproduction can help us understand the ways in which our social lives are folded into this economic system in differentiated ways, and the potential for moving beyond this.

Here, the path-breaking work of scholars like Maria Mies and Silvia Federici has fed contemporary analysis of the work involved in preparing labour power for capital: how feminised, reproductive labour has been integral to the extraction of surplus value from waged, historically masculine workers. Federici's historical work shows how the 'accumulation of differences and divisions within the working class' through the development of capitalism involved the forcible expulsion of women from valorised forms of labour, pushing them into unpaid caring roles that keep 'productive' workers, clothed, fed and familied.[16] This is a racialising as well as gendering process, creating a stratified division of society with women and racialised people at the edges of 'productive' value, incorporated or expelled at different moments depending on the needs of capital. As Cedric Robinson argues in *Black Marxism*, 'the tendency of European civilization through capitalism was ... not to homogenize but to differentiate – to exaggerate regional, subcultural, and dialectical differences into "racial" ones',[17] shoring up wealth and control for dominant elites through slavery, violence and imperialism. Gargi Bhattacharyya demonstrates how this creates 'the edge-populations that serve as the other and limit of the working class', excluding groups of people from both 'productive' labour as defined by capital and the socially reproductive mechanisms that sustain this.[18]

Much feminist scholarship has historically focused on the central role that the nuclear family has played in under-girding these processes – locking women into isolated forms of unpaid, domestic labour whilst literally reproducing the next generation of pliant capitalist subjects. Crucial to our analysis though, is the way that friendship has also played a part in these forms of reproduction and differentiation. How have friendships and interpersonal connections helped sustain these systems? When, like in *Company*, does friendship help paper over the cracks of the nuclear family, or reinforce its exclusionary logic? In a broader sense, friendship often does socially reproductive work similar to that of the family: emotional support, letting off leisurely steam, physically upkeeping idealised bodies through sports and consumption, pulling people into unpaid reproductive labour. At a political level this links to what Emma Dowling calls a contemporary 'care crisis' that is 'intricately linked with the Global Financial Crisis and its aftermath' of austerity, with states compelling people to voluntarily 'care', whilst cutting welfare and formalised care support.[19] Befriending projects for the elderly and a clap-along for NHS workers point to the way in which the decimation of welfare in Britain comes with facile invocations of 'caring' as something 'too valuable' to be properly remunerated.

Such ideas of friendship and care are of course animated by an implicit sense that certain groups of people 'deserve' care in the first place. This is a sentiment that finds particular counter-expression in a range of 'black feminist care ethics',[20] often anchored on Audre Lorde's famous formulation that 'caring for myself is not self-indulgence, it is self-preservation, and that is an act of political warfare'.[21] Sara Ahmed elaborates her own understanding of Lorde's words and work: 'In directing our care towards ourselves we are redirecting care away from its proper objects, we are not caring for those we are supposed to care for, we are not caring for the bodies deemed worth caring about.'[22] Such analysis understands care as a political category in itself: in Lioba Hirsch's words, 'both institutional (and at times violent and antiblack) [and] as that which exceeds and counteracts such instances of violence and exclusion'.[23]

Social life at the 'edges' of capital is necessarily less folded into cycles of production and extraction: 'the labour of remaking human beings against the battering of racial capitalism takes place for the far more usual reasons of love, care, community, survival'.[24] This is not to romanticise what are often very hard and precarious existences, but it is to suggest that we can try and understand something about different forms of care and friendship from those who are excluded from normative social reproduction. This entails pushing back against theories of production and social reproduction that focus more narrowly on 'reproductive' labour as always geared towards the 'productive' worker, from an assumed lack of life 'outside' capital. There are forms of sociality that evade totalising accounts of capitalist capture, as just discussed in reference to O'Brien's work. As Dowling argues:

> Organising on the terrain of social reproduction makes [resistance to capitalism] possible because social reproduction has two dimensions. On the one hand social reproduction pertains to the reproduction of labour power for capitalist exploitation. On the other hand, life is not reducible solely to capitalist command, nor are subjectivities and relationships ever entirely captured and shaped by capital ... In the struggle over social reproduction, it is this contradiction between these two dimensions – of reproducing labour power for capital versus reproducing life itself – that helps to shed light on the possibilities of constructing alternatives.[25]

This leaves us with difficult questions: To what extent are our own friendships and social lives folded into regimes of capitalist reproduction? What would it mean to try and step out of this, whilst acknowledging the differentiated ways in which the system operates? Such questions move us beyond narrow notions of privilege discourse and identity, instead trying to think through ideas of affinity, interconnection and shared vulnerability. If we admit that capital is not complete in its encompassing of our lives, can we find ways to build everyday 'anti-capitalist social reproduction' into more sustained forms of 'insurgent' and 'communist' social reproduction? This involves building critique and discomfort into our relationships: questioning how resources within a friendship group are shared and distributed, what types of care fall on who, how normative social scripts are deployed or left unchallenged. It means questioning why the distribution of caring labour is deeply uneven *within* radical movements today, with women often doing the brunt of work to support people emotionally, care for children and people with other needs, and stick around after the high-profile actions have finished. Challenging these trends may feel partial or small-scale, but it helps push us to let our everyday social lives be grounds for imagining something otherwise. We begin to move away from 'company' towards 'dense bonds' and who knows what else.

This process also requires naming and understanding how normative familial scripts and forms of capitalist social reproduction crop up in our daily lives, and not just within the family itself. But how are family and friendship delineated? And what role have they played in different conceptions of political belonging: fellowship, brotherhood and sisterhood, fraternity, comradeship?

## SLIPPERY KINSHIPS

Friendship is often understood and practised as the inverse of family. People attach dualities to the two concepts that reinforce each of them: friends are voluntarily chosen, families are not; friendship implies sameness (of interests, location, social class) and egalitarian sentiment, families imply an established hierarchy of role and authority; friends are social, families biological. Much early anthropological writing on kinship – the study of how humans organise and make meaning from their social relations – relied on such binaries. In classical colonial anthropology these were combined under the meta-binary of 'West' vs 'Rest', with friendship largely ignored because of an assumption that it was a particular expression of 'Western' individualism. Racist narratives about a serene 'state of nature' were projected onto 'non-Western' groups of people depicted as 'friendly' in disposition, but friendless in social organisation. This was connected to ideas of so-called 'primitive' and 'stateless' societies being organised through ties of blood and marriage, where political organisation and kinship were one and the same, and friendship an expression of 'development' away from this. In the summary of the anthropologist Julian Pitt-Rivers, ironically himself a descendant from a family of well-known anthropologists, 'one tastes the pleasures of friendship only insofar as one has slipped the chains of kinship'.[26] In contrast, in studies of 'modern' societies kinship was 'relegated to the domestic domain' and stripped of 'its economic and political functions', the assumption being that family was incidental to the functioning of enlightened democracy.[27] Friendship didn't fit into either the colonial era kinship diagrams of marriage and lineage, or into related myths about a 'modern' political system free from the influence of kin-based nepotism.

Understanding the actual ways kinship and friendship infuse political life in a whole range of cultural contexts means shedding such assumptions, rooted as they are in racist notions of hierarchy and lineage: that 'Western' democracies are the endpoint of an evolutionary timeline that other 'traditional' societies can aspire to and be violently guided towards.

In recent decades, anthropologists such as David Schneider and Janet Carsten have argued that kinship should be understood within the social and cultural world in which it operates, that blood lines and biology are not preexisting 'natural' facts but culturally contingent ones. As such, they focus more on kinship as a process, on *doing* rather than *being*. Carsten uses the idea of 'relatedness' to understand how people relate, 'without relying on an arbitrary distinction between biology and culture, and without presupposing what constitutes kinship'.[28] Kath Weston's subsequent work on 'chosen families' built on these ideas through a rich ethnography of gay and lesbian kinship in 1990s San Francisco. Weston showed how for such groups building a 'chosen family' wasn't necessarily a rejection of existing familial ties, even where these had been painful, but an attempt to work through and remake these categories.[29] The tension and slippages between family and friendship infuse ideas like 'chosen family' with power, but also risk reinscribing existing binaries and forms of hierarchy. As Weston outlines in the introduction to the paperback edition of *Families We Choose*, kinship can exclude or differentiate even amongst communities that reclaim it: 'Could I begin to take account of race and class differences, while reminding readers just how revolutionary any claim to family is for people not so long ago condemned to the no-mans-land of kinship lost?'[30] Throughout more recent anthropological studies of kinship there is a similar emphasis on how claiming family or friendship is always political, informed by existing power structures and animated by the slippage between seemingly opposed concepts: choice-obligation, friend-family, culture-biology. Rather than natural and essential, these categories themselves are made meaningful by this movement. 'Biology' doesn't make sense outside of the contrasting terms by which we come to know it, the social processes that render it 'fact' and the technological shifts that are folded into it (think for instance about how something like IVF treatment animates and informs what we think of as 'biological family').

Evoking these binaries through a playful hopping between them is also key to many expressions of relation and connection. A vast range of communities draw on blurred familial language in a contrasting sense, from the 'mothers' of queer ballroom culture, to the everyday ways people use 'cousin', 'bro', 'sis' and 'fam'. Gargi Bhattacharyya writes about the idea of the 'Auntie' in South Asian culture as encapsulating much of this slippage, risk and potential:

> Aunties are not always a good thing. All of the unkind gossip and cheek-tugging and dressing down and cruel laughter. On a bad day, aunties can tip you over the edge. But on a good day …
>
> Aunties can be unlike any other grown-up. At once authoritative and iconoclastic. The most monstrous of

self-authoring families, not quite contained by the strict roles of blood and line. A relationship of affinity. Or amusement. Or convenience. In the process showing that all of these things have their place in a human life.[31]

Bhattacharyya goes on to describe a utopian imaginary of the auntie, distinct from her actual experiences of 'aunties' growing up, but informed by the potential these relations implied. The fantasy of family, and its implied opposites, can be as important here as actual (often disappointing, or at worst violent and abusive) realities. A capacity for fantasy is central to utopian imagining of a better world, but it can also mask material limits. Fantasies of both family and political belonging (often hard to disentangle) can push us away from action. As the 'gay communist collective' Pinko argue in the afterword to their collection *After Accountability*, this takes a worrying contemporary political salience in refrains of 'community':

At its worst, community serves as an obscuring fantasy, a fiction we use to psychologically protect ourselves from the horror and despair of life under capitalism. We seize upon a given group of friends, a snapshot of a momentarily vibrant social world, and hope it can last. As it erodes, we set out to find another, or to patch it up where we can.[32]

Grasping to reclaim ideas of 'family', 'friends' and 'community' can certainly be an expression of a lack: of intimacy, collective responsibility, connection, care. In Pinko's analysis, this is fundamentally circumscribed by the totalising force of capital on our social relations. As they argue: 'Because a core activity of collective human life is so absorbed into market relations, non-market relations become hollow, shallow, and fragile. You may love your friends, but you still have to pay rent.'[33] In our reading, however, everyday attempts to try and name sociality and the productive slippages between these can be an important way to manoeuvre towards new forms of social and political belonging. In refusing to settle on established and normative notions of 'family' and 'friend', people start to practise and imagine new kinds of sociality and collective struggle. To do this requires acknowledging the limits of relational 'fantasy' alone, and managing to find commonality through different relational terms. It requires meeting people where they are at in terms of ways of conceiving of commonality, always with an eye on the exclusionary and normative risks of any collective 'we'. Various political movements over time have attempted this task in different ways, instilling forms of political belonging through a range of overlapping kinship terms, whilst also meeting people's material needs.

The rest of this chapter sketches some of these movements in a loose chronology, thinking about the different modes of political belonging and different emotional registers they draw upon. Within many of these examples we find friendship taking on its own conceptual shape at different times. These may involve a juxtaposing, overlapping or outright disavowal of the family, but rarely its complete removal from the picture. However, in her conclusion to *Abolish the Family*, Sophie Lewis advocates for such an absence: 'I can't wait to see what comes after the family. I also know I probably won't see whatever it is. Still, I hope it happens, and I hope it is a glorious and abundant nothing.'[34] The project of family abolition, of which Lewis has been such an important contemporary advocate, critiques the family form as 'the name we use for the fact that care is privatized in our society'.[35] Whereas friendship has often been theorised as a counterpoint to family, it does not feature as such in accounts of family abolition. Like us, writers in this tradition are careful not to assume such binaries. In Lewis's case, the family is the psychic backdrop that limits desires for other kinds of interrelation. As they argue in response to the kinds of 'kin-slippages' we have been discussing:

> When I say to you that you are 'family', or that I think of you as 'kin', I am saying 'I love you, I care for you, I insure you, I hold you, I see you' – yes – and/but I am underlining this by using a metaphor that means I have no real choice about the matter. I am giving you a guarantee (we are kin) tethered to a metaphysical plane. And this feels good! At least, it is supposed to feel good. But obviously, an uncomradely hierarchy is baked right into this entire thought structure. Real kin will always be realer.[36]

As the structuring fantasy of belonging, kinship is always, for Lewis, 'a linguistic appeal to something non-contingent that can ground a relation'.[37] As she asks: 'can we suspend that fantasy of something non-contingent? Can we let go of it?'[38]

Our attraction to friendship is partly because of how it offers a practical, if partial, way of engaging in such letting go, of starting to move away from the prescribed, norma- tive and 'naturalised' bonds of family. As is perhaps now evident, we are less attached to 'abundant nothing' than Lewis, seeing 'kinship' as a politically and socially con- tingent category in-itself.[39] We see the traffic between different expressions of kinship as an everyday process of trying to fumble towards the forms of 'reciprocal care, interdependence, and belonging' that Lewis prioritises.[40] But how have friendship and the familial featured in more formal programmes for political belonging? Where fellowship and fraternity seem marinated in both, is com- radeship somehow different?

## FELLOWSHIPS AND FRATERNITIES, BROTHERS AND SISTERS

As we argued in our Introduction, friendship can cut across time and space. For the nineteenth-century social- ist William Morris, in his novel *A Dream Of John Ball* (1888), John Ball, one of the leaders of the Peasants' Revolt of 1381, reaches out from the fourteenth century to extend the hand of friendship to the revolutionary social- ists of the nineteenth century, proclaiming: 'Fellowship is heaven, and lack of fellowship is hell: fellowship is life, and lack of fellowship is death: and the deeds that ye do upon the earth, it is for fellowship's sake that ye do them.'[41] Ideas of fellowship, and of historical connections *through* fellowship, were woven into many nineteenth-century proto-socialist and socialist movements. Religiosity was often key here, not simply in terms of how practices of 'Christian fellowship' and ideas of shared humanity under

God influenced political movements (some of which were secular), but in the focus on self-improvement, mutual support and the cultivation of 'good character'. The Fellowship of the New Life, a nineteenth-century organisation most famous for its offshoot, the Fabian Society, outlined its aims in minutes from its inaugural 1882 meeting:

> Object: The cultivation of a perfect character in each and all.
> Principle: The subordination of material things to spiritual things.
> Fellowship: The sole and essential condition of fellowship shall be a single-minded, sincere and strenuous devotion to the object and principle.[42]

Members such as the writer and activist Edward Carpenter, animal rights activist Henry Stephens Salt, feminist Edith Lees and the future UK Prime Minister Ramsay MacDonald discussed and practised forms of pacifism, vegetarianism and Tolstoyan asceticism in the society. Clearly influenced by ancient Greek philosophies of brotherly communion, the ideas of 'perfect character' and the focus on individual moral development in such groups could easily tend towards elitism. However, although the advent of more materialist, Marxist analyses of social change swept much of these tendencies aside, we can see residual traces of such sentiments in the valorisation of the 'collective worker' analysed in our Introduction, depicted as a respectable alternative to a demonised lumpenproletariat. It is not an accident that Quakerism, the Protestant Christian movement with a 'priesthood of all believers' (i.e. no established clerical hierarchy), experienced a renaissance around this time. Quaker ideas were threaded into many nineteenth-century conceptions of fellowship, a word used within the faith to denote a particular organisation and set of aims. Quakers famously also refer to each other as 'friends', a reference to John 15:15 in the Bible: 'Henceforth I call you not servants; for the servant knoweth not what his lord doeth: but I have called you friends; for all things that I have heard of my Father I have made known unto you.' Fellowship and friendship here imply an organised commitment to egalitarian spiritual reflection and improvement, and a God that is within and can be drawn upon to enact personal and then social change.

We can see the contemporary influence of fellowship in practices such as consensus decision making, which, though it is rarely introduced as such, has its roots in Quakerism. As the training organisation Seeds for Change explains: 'consensus decision making is a creative and dynamic way of reaching agreement in a group. Instead of simply voting for an item and having the majority getting their way, a consensus group is committed to finding solutions that everyone actively supports – or at least can live with.'[43] L.A. Kauffman traces the history of the practice in a short piece on 'The Theology of Consensus', pointing to a 1976 direct action campaign against Seabrook Nuclear Plant near Boston in the United States. Kauffman describes how:

The organizers ... were eager to find a process that could prevent the pitfalls of structurelessness without resorting to hierarchy. Two staff people from the American Friends Service Committee, the long-standing and widely admired peace and justice organization affiliated with the Society of Friends, or Quakers, suggested consensus.[44]

Though one of the activists, Sukie Rice, explained to Kauffman in a 2002 interview that 'Friends consider [consensus] a waiting upon the Spirit, that you pray that you will do God's will', this wasn't presented as such to the activists, as Quakers try to avoid proselytising.[45] Instead, a secularised version of consensus took hold across many parts of the left, though (as Kauffman points out) sometimes with a level of commitment that borders on the religious.

The desire for methods of organisation that could foreground interpersonal connection and collaborative decision making also animated second wave feminism. In *Beyond the Fragments*, Sheila Rowbotham, Lynne Segal and Hilary Wainwright, well aware of the problems inherent in forms of horizontalism, made clear that interpersonal development was nonetheless central for the women's movement, due to the very nature of patriarchal oppression:

The form in which you choose to organize is not 'neutral' ... If you accept a high degree of centralization ... concentrating above everything upon the central task of seizing power, you necessarily diminish the development of the self-activity and self-confidence of most of the people involved. Because, for the women's movement, the development of this confidence and ability to be responsible for our own lives was felt to be a priority, this became part of the very act of making a movement … We had to learn to love ourselves and other women so we could trust one another without falling back on men. We inclined consequently towards small groups, circles rather than rows, centres as information and research services, open newsletters … the need for our *own* movement and the feeling of sisterhood came from this understanding.[46]

The concept of sisterhood, which gained traction following the publication in 1970 of Robin Morgan's *Sisterhood Is Powerful: An Anthology of Writings from the Women's Liberation Movement*, signalled affective possibilities of feminist collective action and mutual care. It was part of a broader aspirational and optimistic vocabulary of solidarity that animated many global political movements in the 1960s and '70s. Many of these 'appropriated the language of the family to make an argument for collectivity, from the lexicon of kin terms that became the grounds for anticolonial nationalism to the intimate idioms of family in the Civil Rights Movement … reflective of a longer tradition of feminist critiques of the masculine language of "brotherhood"'.[47] The promise of a sisterhood based on common oppression was soon contested by feminists of colour who argued that the idea of common oppression, largely propagated by middle-class white women, 'disguis[ed] and mystifi[ed] the true nature of women's varied and complex social reality'.[48] The concept still had purchase, though, and through these critiques 'sisterhood was reimagined through organizations of writers like "The Sisterhood" with members like Toni Morrison and Alice Walker".[49] Likewise bell hooks, writing in the mid 1980s, argued that 'women do not need to eradicate difference to feel solidarity ... We can be sisters united by shared interests and beliefs, united in our appreciation for diversity, united in our struggle to end sexist oppression, united in political solidarity'.[50]

Across these different examples, fellowship represented an idea of political belonging that appealed to neither nation (like citizenship) nor strict kinship. It captured a certain focus on personal growth and shared interest, as well as a feeling of connectedness, all of which were important to many nineteenth-century political movements. Though fellowship infuses many contemporary political ideologies, it is rarely overtly evoked today. Sisterhood, in all its 'diverse, often contrasting visions of feminist alliance and internationalism', has 'been largely disappeared from today's political movements'.[51] Overlapping ideas of fraternity and brotherhood may be slightly more present in some left-wing discourse, but have had a similar decline in use. Fraters (Latin for brother) and brothers, with their specific reference to gendered kinship roles, are most evident in occasional trade unionist references to 'brothers and sisters' (a friend informs us that some larger union congresses in Britain now also say 'siblings') and in the persistence of 'frat' houses in United States. This was not always so, with the famous French revolutionary triad of 'liberty, equality and fraternity' echoing through various political movements across the nineteenth century. The academic Paul Spicker outlines how:

Fraternity was defined after the French Revolution, in the constitution of year III, in the following terms: 'Do not do to others what you would not want them to do to you; do constantly to others the good which you would wish to receive from them.' The vagueness of the definition suggests that, despite its place in the revolutionary slogan, the idea of fraternity was not clearly understood. This is a version of the 'golden rule', 'do as you would be done by', rather than a radical principle.[52]

Spicker argues that it was the role of actual fraternities – 'guilds, associations and secret societies' – in the revolution which ensured the inclusion of this third (less contemporarily celebrated) pillar.[53] Fraternal orders such as Freemasons, Odd Fellows, clubs for 'gentlemen', and student fraternities in turn have their roots in the organisation of trades and pre-capitalist cities.

In his book *Mutual Aid*, the nineteenth-century Russian Anarchist Peter Kropotkin marvels at the cooperation of medieval guilds in the construction of the Cologne and Basel cathedrals, describing how, despite 'small means' in terms of initial investment, 'each corporation contributed its part of stone, work, and decorative genius to *their* common monument. Each guild expressed in it its political conceptions, telling in stone or in bronze the history of the city, glorifying the principles of "Liberty, equality, and fraternity".[54] Fraternity was about a certain 'common pursuit', not just an idea but a practice of shared activity, usually labour, here enshrined into the built environment. It was also, in all these accounts, about men. Nowhere was this more evident for Kropotkin than on board ships:

Like organizations came into existence wherever a group of men – fishermen, hunters, travelling merchants, builders, or settled craftsmen – came together for a common pursuit. Thus, there was on board ship the naval authority of the captain; but, for the very success of the common enterprise, all men on board, rich and poor, masters and crew, captain and sailors, agreed to be equals in their mutual relations, to be simply men, bound to aid each other and to settle their possible disputes before judges elected by all of them.[55]

In their history of the 'revolutionary Atlantic', Marcus Rediker and Peter Linebaugh quote the English Civil War-era poet Richard Braithwaite making a similar claim. He describes the seventeenth-century mariner as such: 'Stars cannot be more faithful in their society than these Hans-kins in their fraternity. They will have it valiantly when they are ranked together, and relate their adventures with wonderful terror.'[56] Sailors were tightly bound by the terms of their profession, the cultural forms that emerged alongside this (shanties and songs), and the particular 'pidgin' languages they forged to communicate amongst themselves. Fraternity was perhaps most evident amongst pirates and maroons, who established communal ways of living both on land and at sea. Rediker and Linebaugh go on to describe how these 'multiracial' 'motley crews', brought together in the ports, shipyards and cities of a pre-capitalist Atlantic, exhibited threatening kinds of kinship: 'Solidarity was not restricted to the genetic nuclear family, nor could it be so restricted among "outcasts". As Francis [a Black servant woman and anabaptist in seventeenth-century Bristol] spoke of the "sisters" of her spiritual community, so the Irish soldiers called one another "brother".[57] Formed through shared activity and everyday solidarity, this was a different kind of mutuality to that of the 'Fellowships' sketched above, though many groups drew on the languages of both. All were infused with ideas and practices of what we would now call friendship, often with a particular focus on forming shared sentiments between people through mutual activity. All were also influential in the dominant emerging idea of revolutionary belonging at the end of the nineteenth century: the comrade.

## COMRADES

Fellowship and fraternity, brotherhood and sisterhood, all drew on notions of the familial then, along with ideas and practices of friendship, in both radical and exclusionary ways. Ideas of comradeship built upon these notions, at times also involving a radical critique of the family form. The historical advent of comradeship coincided with the emergence of an organised workers' movement across Europe and North America, yet there is no neat overlap between the 'collective worker' and the 'comrade'. Jodi Dean's passionate defence of the comrade as idea, practice and 'necessary condition for communism' traces the history of the word's ascendance in vivid detail.[58] Interestingly, in Dean's account, these origins are quite removed from the experiences and practices of industrial workers. Instead, she traces how middle-class, ethically focused socialists in England and the United States were drawn to the poet Walt Whitman's 'vision of ... deep fellowship and interconnectedness' in searching for a new language that could move beyond the filial limits of brotherhood and fraternity.[59]

Dean draws on the historian Kirsten Harris's investigations into the journal *Justice* – where 'the first socialist evocation of comradeship written in English' appears in 1884 – and the 1901–5 journal *The Comrade*, which threaded Whitman's 'homoeroticism, homosociality, and celebratory queerness' into its depictions of 'manly love' between comrades.[60] Dean quotes a 1903 edition of *The Comrade*, in which W. Harrison Riley 'recounted some of his encounters with Marx (whom he said "was as good to look at as to listen to" and "well built and remarkably good looking")', before observing that 'the Internationalists addressed each other as "Citizen", but I disliked the designation and frequently substituted Whitman's greeting, "Comrade"'. Marx was quick to adopt the term too, specifically to designate a political affinity and shared struggle within the complex threads of the internationalist movement. Dean illuminates various aspects of the comrade, some of which overlap with the fellowships and fraternities previously outlined: shared activity, 'manly' intimacy, self-improvement, ethical accountability to one another. Other aspects have a different quality: the link to 'comrades in arms' suggests a particular binding through organised violence and war, while the idea of discipline within an organised political party starts to take shape.

That the comrade took on a sometimes homoerotic, queer quality, often evoked in contemporary family abolitionist writing, links to its use in overt communist

critiques of the family. In outlining the *Communist Man-
ifesto*'s 'infamous proposal' – 'Abolition of the family!'
– Marx and Engels make it clear that they see the abolition
of the bourgeois family and the abolition of private property as intrinsically linked. They understood bourgeois
families as the units through which capitalism organised and drastically limited the ownership of property to
a powerful few, as well as the internal logics of property
that functioned within such families: parents owned children, husbands owned wives. Figures such as Alexandra
Kollontai, communist revolutionary and briefly 'People's
Commissar for Social Welfare' in the first Soviet government of 1917, advanced such critiques in profound ways.
Kollontai's 1920 pamphlet 'Communism and the Family'
argues for comradeship as a way to move beyond the
limits of familial unit: 'In place of the individual and egois-
tic family, a great universal family of workers will develop,
in which all the workers, men and women, will above all
be comrades.' As the editors of a collection of Kollontai's
writing outline, her definition of comradeship entailed
plurality and, specifically, 'red' or 'comradely love':

> Kollontai thus envisions a social love defined by multi-
> plicity along two axes: a love of many in many ways. On
> the first axis, beyond the bounds of those who are yours
> – the couple, the family, the identity, the people – she
> urges us to develop bonds with a wide range of people,
> developing forms of love-comradeship and love-soli-
> darity. 'The "sympathetic ties" between all the members
> of the new society' will have to grow and be strength-
> ened. The qualities and intensities of these diverse

attachments, obviously, will not be the same. On the second axis, then, one must develop 'many and varied bonds of love and friendship'.[61]

However, while Dean also argues for the comrade's power to disrupt 'family, heteropatriarchy, and binary gender', she notes the different ways in which this was contested.[62] In the communist parties of both the US and USSR, the 'early Soviet experiments in dismantling bourgeois familial and sexual norms' typified by Kollontai gave way through the 1930s to more conservative ideas of the family, emphasising women's roles in nurturing 'a new generation of class-conscious communists'.[63] In this instance, comradeship's ability to contain or condition the family is determined by the party line, reducing abundant 'red love' to something far greyer.

Dean describes the comrade as 'a figure of political belonging, term of address, and carrier of expectations for action'.[64] Throughout her account, she emphasises the powerful ways in which experiences of comradeship could bind people in collective action, making them feel charged with possibility and joy. She recounts the 'political purpose' and 'life-giving capacity' that Communist Party members experienced through comradeship, often drawing on Vivian Gornick's *The Romance of American Communism*. Yet as Hannah Proctor argues, in a discussion of the emotional aftermath of political breakdowns within such movements: 'the grandiose explanations of the world that infused communist and feminist lives with meaning, expansive elation and transformative solidarity, were, for Gornick, also the origins of dogmas that caused people to demand impossible standards of behaviour from themselves and others'.[65] Dogma is not intrinsic to the comrade, but it certainly came to define it for many who lived through these movements.

In Chinese usage, the equivalent to comradeship, *tongzhi* (meaning 'common will' or 'common aspiration'), encapsulates such a shift. Many historical accounts point to the revolutionary leader and first president of the People's Republic, Sun Yat-sen, popularising *tongzhi* as a word signalling shared revolutionary commitment and party membership. The American sociologist Ezra Vogel argued in a 1965 article that from 1950 onwards *tongzhi* took on increasing prominence in everyday Chinese society, eclipsing friendship.[66] Vogel argues that people were mistrustful of personal intimacy and of inviting people into their homes, worrying that private information might be passed to state authorities, or that they might be accused of not adhering to good communist practice. Subsequent studies have highlighted the declining use of the term in everyday Chinese life, particularly from the 1980s onwards, by which time 'comradeship had vanished as a central ethic holding the fabric of Chinese society together'.[67] Paul Joscha Kohlenberg argues that 'the Party leadership from Mao Zedong to Xi Jinping has also turned to the "comrade" salutation during campaigns, inspections, and purges as a supplementary political tool',[68] as the invocation of insufficient or improper 'comradeship' is used in 'anti-corruption' drives to discipline those deemed disloyal. A 2015 article in *Study Times* (*Xuexi shibao*), a newspaper of the Central Party School of the Chinese Communist Party, reaffirmed the importance of party members using the word 'comrade' as part of President Xi Jinping's continued fight to combat the 'four bad work styles' of 'formalism, bureaucracy, hedonism, and extravagance'.[69] In more recent years, *tongzhi* has become widely used in China and neighbouring regions as a term of belonging for the LGBTQ+ community, resonating with the nascently queer Whitmanite uses we outlined earlier.

The active use of 'comrade' in anglophone contexts today is generally reserved to some segments of the trade union movement, Trotskyist and Stalinist groups, and a scattered selection of 'small c' communist tendencies. Though many still attempt to instil comradeship as practice and ethic, the word also offers a way to signal one's fealty to particular readings of communist history, a linguistic version of a little red flag lapel badge. In Britain, through the ascendency and eventual defeat of Corbynism, usage of the word seemed to grow again within broader left-wing scenes, but with a different quality to that which Dean identifies. In this context, it's not unusual to hear people introduced or spoken about as 'a good comrade', in ways synonymous to discussions of someone having 'good politics'. Comrade becomes a shorthand for common ground, but without the association of party membership or even an agreed shared commitment to a particular set of political strategies. Dean is adamant in contrasting comradeship with 'allyship', which she argues works as an individuated set of techniques for managing discomfort and making self-improvements 'without any organized political struggle at all'.[70] Yet this particular contemporary use of 'comrade' often does similar work to 'the ally' in that it signals politics-as-identity through mutual interpellation, usually through an assumed (and sometimes not much discussed) reading of political history and strategy. The historical resonances that attract some people to the contemporary use of 'comrade' can of course be incredibly off putting to others, particularly if they come from parts of the world where the word has a more hardened, authoritarian meaning. Noticing such limits doesn't necessarily mean abandoning the word entirely, but any attempt to recast comradeship in the way Dean hopes to must surely reckon with its actual contemporary usage as well as the historical weight it carries.

Radical organising today requires specificity and multiplicity – it may involve the comrade, but it cannot be reduced to only this. We need comradeship without 'the comrade' as we know it, infused with friendship and its capacity to focus us on practice, plurality and interpersonal connection. We need to build from people's existing experiences of interconnection, to politicise these forms of sociality and figure new ways of naming and sustaining this. Many of the most inspiring organising drives of the last two decades – from tenant unions, climate youth strikes and neighbourhood anti-raids groups to worker organising by delivery drivers, nurses, teachers and sex workers – have highlighted specific forms of political proximity and sociality to advance broader critiques. Popular contemporary strategies of workplace organising such as Jane McAlevey's 'social movement' and worker-fronted model look to build 'organic leaders among the masses of ordinary people', specifically through a focus on social skills, embedding action within the community and connecting to people's interpersonal lives.[71] Such movements start from everyday experiences, deploying terms of belonging and shared activity that people already use ('neighbour', 'nurse', 'mother') and building from there. In contrast, for Dean, the comrade 'does not eliminate difference', but is 'a container indifferent to its contents' – including other relational forms: 'friendship, kinship, citizenship, neighbor'.[72] Here, friendship, which Dean is suspicious of as cliquish, 'closed and unwelcoming' (surely an issue for 'comrades' too!), needs to be 'contained' by the disciplining forces of comradeship, which 'requires a degree of alienation from the needs and demands of personal life to which friends must attend'.[73] But how does one divide the personal from the political in such instances? Who arbitrates which needs are which?

Central to Dean's argument is the organisational and binding role of the political party, a body made up of the cellular nodes of 'comrade', and the unit by which this relation is prescribed: 'one doesn't choose one's comrades. The collective does.' There is no comrade without the party in such an account, leaving the question of who constitutes the 'collective' after the decline of the mass communist parties unanswered. This is a vision quite different to that of early communist family abolitionists like Kollontai. In her 1923 piece 'Make Way for Winged Eros: A Letter to Working Youth', Kollontai not only advocates for gender equality, mutual respect, and love beyond property and ownership, but also for 'comradely sensitivity', an 'ability to listen and understand the inner workings of the loved person'.[74] Kollontai's vision of 'comradely love' calls for personal, political and interpersonal transformation, a solidarity that not only entails 'awareness of common interests' but 'depends also on the intellectual and emotional ties linking the members of the collective'.[75]

## *HEVALTÎ*

Personal, political and interpersonal transformations of the kind described by Kollontai are happening now, and these practices are creating new political realities. In the Autonomous Administration of North and East Syria, also known as Rojava, friendship underpins the revolutionary regime. Influenced by the writings of its founder, Abdullah Öcalan, the Kurdistan Workers' Party (PKK) defines itself as an organisation of relationships that transform people into revolutionary subjects. Friendship, or *hevaltî* in Kurdish, names the accumulated perspective and knowledge gained through this process. In the PKK's view, 'it is in the company of friends that one journeys toward collective truth and freedom. Friendship is a form of loyalty that cannot be contained within nation, property, or household. It cannot be transformed into utility and cannot be exchanged. It involves both equality and differentiation'.[76]

In other words, in Rojava, 'friendship [is] a genre of humanity'.[77] Here, friendship designates a particular form of self-cultivation; friendship gives militants and guerrillas in Rojava a rhythm, a set of everyday habits, and 'affectively inculcates [their] orientation towards the world'.[78] In this way, practices of friendship, as we seek to argue in this book, bridge the prosaic and the profound: 'friendship is both a push that forces the guerrilla to move beyond herself and a pull that grounds her sociality, anchors and sustains her. It is a form of being and becoming.'[79] Like Foucault's understanding of friendship as a way of life, militants in Rojava reject filial society and familial forms of social reproduction. These guerrillas, many of whom were born and raised in a traditional filial society, find themselves in a state (not unlike that of queer communities) where they must transform how they relate to one another and 'redefine their mutual dependencies and duties'.[80] A commitment to *hevaltî*, therefore, is the necessary precondition through which activists and militants in Rojava are able to commit to forms of criticism and self-criticism and to formulate new social contracts. Friendship forms an essential foundation and a self-defence mechanism for the organising structure to function.

Importantly then, in Rojava, friendship is not simply a concept of study, but rather a practice that is made and remade on a daily basis. As the philosopher David Webb puts it, 'friends are those with whom we work on the historical conditions of our existence, and those with whom we share the practice of becoming who we are'.[81] For most of us, living under capitalism, such bonds of being and belonging can often feel marginal at best. Elif Sarican and Dilar Dirik argue in 'Rallying the Commons' that attempts to build communities based on solidarity, mutual aid and collective care 'often collapse under the weight of capitalism's fragmenting and individualising logics. Initiatives, therefore, often remain small in scale or survive at the margins of society.'[82] The practice of *hevaltî*, therefore, has much to offer us. In Rojava, friendship is prefiguration, practice and promise. Sarican and Dirik suggest that:

the liberal notion of 'tolerance' that 'we don't have to like each other, we just have to be able to get the work done' is a damaging one that opens up communities to infiltration and attacks from the state. Of course, no method or mechanism is inherently impenetrable – but we wonder whether community and organising structures were based on an understanding that 'if we are fighting together, we need to try and like, in fact, love each other, too', they would be safer and more sustainable.[83]

Sarican and Dirik's insistence on love, in defiance of a political system which demands calm (often cruel) rationality, challenges us to consider friendship as a powerful means by which to cut through hollow utterances of comradeship and community, and instead to actually do it, to live it! Friendship is often made to seem immature or naive in the realm of 'serious' political thinking – we are encouraged to tolerate harm and to be grown up and stay cool-headed even when we disagree. But Leela Gandhi, writing about anti-colonial friendship networks at the turn of the twentieth century, reminds us that under such conditions, friendship, as an 'immature' gesture of refusal and relationality, can be radical precisely because it 'struggle[s] against the profound contradiction at the heart of modern political life – diagnosed by thinkers like Hannah Arendt and more recently Giorgio Agamben – by which the "mature" promise of collectivity, solidarity, and inclusion is premised perversely upon a logic of caesura, exception, and exclusion'.[84] In other words, sometimes attempts to categorise or define forms of political belonging only serve to reify exclusion. Friendship, though, is not easily codified or contained. All of the forms of political belonging we've discussed here have been animated by forms of friendship in one way or another, and if we choose to recognise friendship by its multiform practices – as an 'ability to listen and understand the inner workings of the loved person', as Kollontai said[85] – rather than by strict demarcation, then we might discover in it a rich resource for something yet to come!

*   *   *

As we've seen throughout this chapter, friendship can be a hollowed out and capitalistic thing: whether a *Company*-esque mirror to normative ideas of marriage and family, or a socially reproductive glue that helps sustain capitalist systems. Family abolitionist analysis can illuminate these processes, as well as helping us think about the historical ways in which political movements have attempted to reconfigure their terms of collective belonging. Perhaps counterintuitively though, rather than fully dismissing 'family' and 'friendship' (always in a productive tension) as useful grounds for political organising, we can instead see how important they have been for revolutionary struggle, pointing towards existing practices of anti-capitalist sociality and everyday solidarity, along with new and unknown forms of relationality for the future.

# Conversation with Gargi Bhattacharyya

*Joel and Laura met Gargi Bhattacharyya while putting together this book (Gargi edits the Pluto Fireworks series), having crossed paths at a few events beforehand. Gargi lives and works in London and writes about racism, racial capitalism, austerity and war. This is an edited version of a conversation that took place online in December 2024, as we were finishing the book.*

**Joel**: Hi Gargi. I wanted to start by asking if you think it's important that people like each other, or 'get along', in political movements? Is that friendship?

**Gargi**: I think that what you are doing in this book, looking at a series of historical case studies of how people have 'got along' in liberation movements, might offer a bigger repertoire of ways of being with each other. Beyond: 'be nice', or 'be polemical'. Because we need different, more precise modes of communication. For instance, comradely letter writing is a form of hard political debate, but it's not the kind of hard political debate that we see in a public meeting, where part of the point is to take up space so others come with you. It's a different kind of dialogic process. And of course, there's a huge part of the left's history, and our ability to intellectualise the world, which has come from such correspondence between people. And a lot of the theoretical kind of intricacies are played out between them, not in the same shouty way that you do when you denounce people, but not at all sugary either.

I also think there's a different aspect to this question of whether we need to be 'nice' or 'polemical' in our politics. It's about a sadness or hardness that comes from facing the horror of the world. Because, lately, the horror has only moved closer and higher in our consciousness, making it uncomfortable to feel the pleasures and comforts and joys of everyday life. I think it feels very, very difficult at the moment. My friends and I, we all have that sense that the small comforts you can be to each other aren't really available, because it's too much. To be people who believe in liberation is to be people who know the horror we currently live in.

**Joel**: Absolutely. And that links to my next question. Because something we've tried to articulate in the book is about the degree to which that system, and its horrors, conditions our sociality. The degree to which it is totalising. So, how do we build political belonging in the face of capitalist totality, in the face of what you've called 'the death machine'?

**Gargi**: I think firstly, it's important sometimes to say really obvious things to each other, because otherwise it's too impossible to keep going, isn't it? So, of course, we know that capitalism is a totalising system that impinges on every aspect of our life and all our social relations. But, within that totalisation it also operates by allowing us, or even encouraging us, to have all kinds of odd idiosyncrasies, illusory kinds of autonomy. And even if these are illusory, what can happen there is not altogether predict-able or decided.

So, then it's a question: When we think about friend-ship, in this really quite brutalising system, does it matter that some of our modes of care and fun and play with each other are also subject to commodification? And you know I don't really think it matters. I'm not looking for a clean friendship that is untouched by capitalist power, that's unimaginable to me. Maybe we all can only play in the park given to us by capitalism, but the games we play always have elements of innovation, and talking back and turning.

**Joel**: How do you think this relates to questions of social reproduction, and do you think these processes have changed over the last two decades?

**Gargi**: Well, I do think that friendship is part of the kind of basket of practices of social reproduction, it seeps into the material. We saw this during Covid, that even things like who can eat and heat can be mediated or reorganised through friendship, or that it can be a kind of safety net.

But a lot of what friendship has done in the last couple of decades of capitalism has been a remaking of the social as far more fragmented, far more online, far more indi-viduated, far more disembodied. And these forms of friendships come with their own pleasures and all kinds of very interesting connections. Friendship becomes a mode of social reproduction which allows us just enough human contact to keep going.

This shift has also influenced some of the knee-jerk rejections of friendship we see, along with the moves back towards Leninism or the revolutionary party. Whereas I think this should be a chance to really interrogate what our terms of sociality are, what our terms of collectivity are, and to reimagine what different kinds of political vehicles might be apt for our moment. And accepting this probably means having a number of different vehicles.

**Joel**: Yes, and that again takes us into the next question nicely. Because part of the issue here is the failure to learn from past struggles and to make links that are intergenerational, or inter-anything really. So: how has intergenerational friendship shaped your own engagement with struggle?

**Gargi**: Firstly, I am famously into intergenerational collaboration. One of the things that capitalism does to us is it divides us into mainly age-based cohorts in different ways. It splits our life course into a series of highly commodified chapters and segments. It concocts us as a market, which tends to be age horizontal, and it does that because that really works in terms of the reproduction of the machine, and it closes our collective ability to understand what it is to reproduce humanity. So, it kind of cuts: the child, the adolescent, the parent, the midlife, etc. It's a commodified lifespan that determines when you're allowed to be mates and when you're meant to retreat into biological reproduction.

And for us as a movement, it's not the main prize, but it's part of the journey, I think, for us to find ways to be together that confound those logics. It's easier said than done, but I think it's really worth a try, and I think you hear far more people now talking explicitly about that.

I think some of that – because, we are creatures of our time, and some of it, because people are just nice – can be a bit oddly stultified. It's focused around: 'Listen to the young people. Learn from our elders.' You know, I've been in some of that stuff. But this is not really an interaction, is it? It's like a mutual performance. 'This is what the young think.' 'This is what the old people remember.' Well, that might be a practice run. But that's not the thing. Let us try and imagine ways of being in which we do not think of each other as repositories or resources in such a blatant, uncomfortable way.

Despite that, I do think even those things, they allow contact, don't they? And once people have met each other, then all kinds of unexpected things can happen and do happen. I partly became a 'movement auntie', if I am recognised as that by anyone but myself, through being a parent. Because being a parent means you're in political space very differently. It means that either you absent yourself for a while, or your kids are being cared for by other people, which most people can't manage and don't want anyway. Because the things we do to stay alive take so many of our hours. We don't want more hours taken from the time we can be with our children.

If you're not that, then you're in political spaces where there's different kinds of need, frailty, accommodation, collaboration. Different, unexpected friendships that arise.

So of course, there's all kinds of people I know, who are quite a lot younger than me, that I know because they played – not as children themselves but in a mixed group – with my children when they were very young. And now they're slightly older adults, and my children are big teenagers. But something else has been sewn together about who we can be to each other, because we've been in spaces where we're trying to do something political. But this other sociability was necessary for us to even be able to be in the space, and I think that is also part of intergenerational solidarities. I hope, as I rush into older parts of my life, that it goes the other way as well, but I think maybe we're less practised at that.

Of course, aging changes our physical needs and ability to be in different spaces. And responding to that is part of our learning together that 'we' is our collective energies, capacities, powers and endeavours. And for that 'we' to be anything close to powerful and extensive and mobile enough to meet the challenges ahead of us, that intergenerational buoying up in different ways – physical, emotional, friendship, skill sharing, keeping an eye out – will be vital. It's part of what needs to be practised and celebrated.

**Joel**: Absolutely. That's beautiful. Do you think friendship gets harder as we get older?

**Gargi**: Well, I think it's important to admit that I, in common with all kinds of people across the left, find friendship extremely hard generally. I find it very, very hard to be with other people. I know it's necessary, but it's not my space of ease.

I'm not the life and soul. Probably most of us are not. And as we've said, even those amongst us who are more conventionally sociable – the weight of the horror that our politics puts us in an encounter with, it ripples through our relations with other people. It's about comprehending where we are and what is before us. It is, I'm afraid, almost certainly part of revolutionary consciousness, and probably always has been.

Part of wishing to be part of that absolute transformation is that you're not the top of anyone's 'going down the pub list'! Because however hard we work on not being scoldy, not being po-faced, not giving a lecture, just the fact of being involved in trying to change the world, for people who are not yet involved, our presence is a reminder that another world is possible, but has to be fought for, and that reminder is painful. And I think that can really cut social relations.

I think it's also well known that middle-aged and older people tend to have a very small number of friends that they have known for a very, very long time. And as you get older some of them die, and people are not around. So, I am fearful of what the ability to have revolutionary friendship or any friendship as I get older and older might be. I also think that is a kind of collective challenge for us all to think about.

We're living a lot longer. So, it used to be people got very, very lonely, but they died soon. Well, now it might be very, very lonely, and live for another 30 years. People's minds are blown. They're quite rightly blown, because we don't have a script! It used to be: 'be a kid, have some fun for a while. Date, then have a partnership. Do a lot of housework. And then at the end, go on a cruise and die.' But as things stand, for some of us, it'll be a long cruise!

So, I know I'm terrified, but I'm not the only one who's terrified. And the things people are terrified of – it sounds horrible – but is an opportunity for the left, isn't it? Because the hot terror gives us a clue as to where people's hearts are, what their needs are.

One of my many half-baked schemes is to start a Communist Old People's Home. Somewhere where you could do some painting and pottery if you want. But then we'd have intensive reading groups and visiting speakers, and then we'd eat together in the night. I think I might do it as an experiment! And we need experiments in other ways of being together, they must be part of what we're building. Otherwise, why would anyone come with us? Otherwise, it feels impossible, doesn't it? You've got to kind of practise a bit!

# CHAPTER TWO

## *Work Friends*

### FRIEND FIRST, BOSS SECOND

There are lots of differences between Ricky Gervais's David Brent and Steve Carrell's Michael Scott, the central 'boss' characters in the mockumentary series *The Office* in its original British and subsequent American iterations. Brent is brittle, deeply unlikeable, creepy. Scott is depicted as sympathetic, naively childlike, an inept father-figure for a workplace that viewers are invited to see as a lovable, if sometimes infuriating, family home. It is telling that it was the latter series which continued to grow in popularity after its (universally panned) final series in 2013. This was heightened through the Covid-19 pandemic: according to the market researchers Nielsen, the show racked up a total of 57.1 billion minutes in 2020 in the US alone, towering over any rivals.[1]

*The (American) Office*'s tone of sweetness, comfort, routine and proximity – often through 'reaction shots' that let the viewer into the frame (whilst also anticipating 'memeifcation') – clearly appealed to millions of people. Though some may have been nostalgic for a specific experience of office life, most were instead enchanted by an imaginary of work that provided friendship, romance, gentle drama and the stability of school-like routine, from daily coffees to Christmas parties. Gen Z pop star

Billie Eilish, whose song 'My Strange Addiction' features samples from the series, spoke of watching the entire 201-episode series fourteen times: a re-watching routine *of* routines shared by many who would never have experienced 'office life' as such.[2] Similarly, a friend of Joel's told him that she put the show on in the background every night, to help her get to sleep. *The Office* buries a celebratory ethic of work – as redemptive, necessary and fulfilling – beneath a veneer of anti-work and a particular aesthetic of ordinariness. This is epitomised by Jim, the apparent everyman-prankster-slacker who viewers are constantly reminded is secretly good at his job, a job he admits constitutes his identity. As he states in the show's finale, 'everything I have I owe to this job – this stupid, wonderful, boring, amazing job'.

In gaining appeal, *The Office* clearly lost some of the satirical edge of its original British counterpart, however limited that satire may have been. Brent's famous declaration in the original season of the show, 'I'm a friend first and a boss second, probably an entertainer third', is presented as evidence of his hubris and ridiculousness: bosses and workers can't be friends. On this fact both human resources handbooks and trade union organising strategies would seem to agree. Yet the appeal of *The Office* in both its iterations rests in part on the frictions of socialising through and within work. Something about turning up, clocking on and falling in-and-out of forced social groups appealed to viewers, especially when this was interrupted by stay-at-home directives and social distancing public health measures. *The (American) Office* depicts a workplace infused with friendships between apparently ordinary people, friendships which the producers deliberately aimed to paint as 'real', in contrast with the laugh-tracked sociality and Hollywood good looks of *Friends* and *Cheers*. In this apparent devotion to 'reality' (as mundanity), the show anticipates actual reality television. But when television turns up in actual workplaces, it's far harder to maintain such genial tones.

From the glamourous bitching of *Selling Sunset*'s LA brokerage office, to the 24/7 luxury yacht service work of the *Below Deck* franchise, social relations in workplace reality TV are marked by friction, resentment and occasional shagging. The contrast with *The Office* is perhaps best exemplified by the largely forgotten 2013 BBC3 series *The Call Centre*, in which 'real-life David Brent' Nev Wilshire runs 'Swansea's third-largest call centre'. 'Big Nev', seemingly lacking Brent's desire to be liked and respected by his employees, famously starts each day with a mass singalong. In one scene he barks at a visibly uncomfortable office room: 'On your feet then! We sing! Mr Brightside, The Killers, C#', because 'miserable bastards don't sell, happy people sell, and happy people sing'. A cruel inversion of the history of workplace singing and work songs as ways to pass time and feel camaraderie with fellow workers, such moments show how enforced forms of sociality and sentiment are used by bosses and managers to increase productivity and dull dissent. These kinds of TV shows present waged work not just as moral and meritocratic, but as deeply social. Performance in 'the team' is one aspect of this, but in a more profound way all such shows implore us to let work condition our social lives, to surrender our sociality and emotions to a system of exploitation and extraction. Work, and infusing portions of our social and emotional lives with work, becomes an ethical prerogative.

In this sense, workplace TV follows a parallel (and well-documented) trend in reality shows of the 2000s, which the writer Jason Okundaye characterises as marked by the class-stratified demonisation of non-work:

> Gameshows, reality television, and comedies were the central genres of mainstream public broadcast which offered up those seeking fame, financial prosperity, or interventions in their personal lives for ritual humiliation to gratify middle-class attitudes towards lower social classes. Blairism's regular attacks on 'scroungers', 'chavs', single mothers, asylum seekers, and hooded youths provided a sheen of respectability to TV executives who made a career out of mocking Britain's most marginalised, allowing it to become a pursuit of popular culture.[3]

Such shows attacked not only a certain idea of 'unproductivity', but the social lives people labelled 'unproductive' might attempt to enjoy. Such attacks have barely paused in the last two decades, with Prime Minister Keir Starmer's 2024 statements about the 'bulging benefits bill blighting our society' being just one recent example.[4] Government narratives around benefits continually mandate 'looking for work' alongside punishments for engaging in activities deemed 'non-work'. Of course, this takes heightened form when dealing with people excluded from work on immigration or other grounds, with 'unproductivity' operating as a threat. Expressions of 'unproductive' sociality, racialised and racialising, become a source of prying intrigue and state intervention. And work, across all these cultural examples, becomes a precondition for sociality.

\* \* \*

This chapter is about the complex intersections of work and friendship. Workplaces have always been key sites of interconnection, solidarity and co-conspiracy, with many people experiencing profound emotional and political connections through struggles within and against work. As the examples above show, there is also a certain fantasy of work that appeals to many: the workplace as convivial, caring and imbued with small, unthreatening acts of idleness and rebellion. That this is so far from most people's experiences of work does not seem to dampen the sense of yearning, not least because work takes up such a disproportionate amount of people's time. Here, sociality – from forced everyday camaraderie to organised 'work nights out' – is drawn upon by bosses in ways far more insidious than David Brent's bad dancing. Yet the power of a close ally and friend at work can cut through this: making things bearable, pointing to other ways of being, building towards collective struggle. Relationships are rarely clear-cut in this sense either; the boundary of work/non-work, of figuring out when friendships and social life are being instrumentalised towards profit, is not always explicit. This is complicated further when we investigate the deeper structures of differentiation – separating people across lines of class, race, gender and other social categories – that pivot on ideas of 'productivity'. As Gargi Bhattacharyya argues, 'the perceived boundary between work and non-work goes to the heart of the practices of differentiation for exploitation and expropriation that make up racial capitalism'.[5] The structural exclusion of groups of people from paid and/or legal work, and the ways in which certain kinds of activity are deemed 'non-work', influences ideas of friendship and social life across the board.

The chapter begins by looking at the historical ways in which trade unions and other organisations have attempted to build solidarity across different types of 'productivity', as well as often entrenching such divisions in exclusionary ways. Histories of workplace organising often paint a picture of trade unions emerging through the efforts of sedentary, locally clustered industrial workers, creating organising problems for the far more diffuse, mobile and digital workforces we see today. We problematise some of the assumptions which guide such narratives, showing how movement, informal friendships and other forms of sociality not captured by formalised trade union and party structures were also key to the development of working-class struggle. The chapter then considers the blurring of work and friendship in contemporary life, looking at questions of emotional labour and what we term 'ambient friendship'.

## CO-CONSPIRACY AT WORK

Work and friendship are inextricably bound together in the symbols, slogans and iconography of the trade union movement (handshakes galore!). This history shows both the long and determined enthusiasm for combination and collectivity in the workplace, and also the ways in which these forms of unity have forever been constrained by precisely the powerful interests they seek to keep in check.

Workers combining to protect their interests has a long history. Modern forms of combination, in contrast to the medieval guild system (which oversaw craft production but included both workers *and* masters), emerged in the eighteenth century to represent the interests of workers alone, particularly within skilled trades such as tailoring, carpentry and printing. By the late eighteenth century, industrialisation was causing increasing numbers of skilled workers – fearing job losses from mechanisation and automation – to combine. The growth of manufacturing and commerce under a capitalist system meant that although the number of skilled workers in the economy was increasing, the opportunity for these workers to advance from journeyman to master was declining. The rising demand for their labour, coupled with their evolving role as long-term waged employees, as well as the gradual retreat of the state from wage regulation and broader labour market intervention, were key in the early development of labour organisation. At the same time, ideas coming out of the American, French and Haitian revolutions were infusing many workplaces with notions of equality and fraternity and prompting questions about the parity and sustainability of industrial capitalism. Fearful of revolutionary unrest, Prime Minister William Pitt passed the Combinations Acts (in 1799 and 1800), making it illegal for two or more workers to combine for the purposes of obtaining higher wages or reducing hours of work.

Histories of early trade union organising often paint a picture of settled, similar and self-regulating workers combining to fight common oppressions. Malcolm Chase shows how, in the early nineteenth century, 'the language, hierarchy and inner life of workers associations reflected their perception of themselves as self-regulating communities, bound in an allegiance to "the trade" as strong as any they might also have felt to place', so that 'even where occupational and residential communities were not homogeneous a significant degree of overlap was usual in this period. Most workers continued to live in the vicinity of their work.' Unions, therefore, were also likely to 'shad[e] off into the other self-help initiatives, the pubs where they met, the local communities in which they were situated and the inner life of the workplace itself'.[6] This could make unionising, and even access to solidarity, difficult for transient or seasonal workers.

Indeed, in many of the most evocative twentieth-century examples of robust trade union culture (for example, in the National Union of Mineworkers), work, leisure and wider community sociality are inextricably linked. 'Mining communities were vibrant communities, but they were built around the pit. The pit was the heart of the community, it was the pit that bound everyone together', recalls one NUM leader, Chris Kitchen. 'The code of honour that existed underground was part of the fabric of the community as well. You didn't get young lads going off the rails at the weekend. You wouldn't upset an old guy because he would be the same one you'd rely on in the pit to protect your life at work, so why would you upset him at the weekend over a few pints?'[7] Histories of the NUM help to sustain some of the most durable mythologies of union organising (particularly because of the viciousness with which the state sought to smash it during the 1984/5 strike) and continue to point to a model of workplace friendship that is all-encompassing, settled and well established.

However, these romantic visions often paper over the exclusionary and narrow visions of friendship enacted through trade unions, particularly for those marginalised due to racism or ableism. In the latter half of the nineteenth century and into the twentieth, unions across the British Empire and the Americas were complicit in producing and reproducing ideologies of white labourism.

The abolition of slavery in the British Empire in the 1830s caused plantation owners and colonial bureaucracies to turn to indentured labour, largely from India and China. This drove down wages and made the use of cheap labour a key target for unions. In making their arguments, unions compounded the racialisation of workers across the Empire, in ways that feel very familiar today. The demonisation of low-waged and indentured workers and sailors (referred to as 'coolies' and 'lascars' respectively – derogatory terms originating in the sixteenth century to designate workers of Asian, Chinese, or Arab descent) was increasingly deployed by workers, union leaders and labour politicians to instil suspicion in white workers and to degrade attempts to forge international worker solidarities. Kornel Chang has shown how 'the notion of white racial destiny and entitlement fueled the labor politics of anti-Asian agitation in the Pacific Northwest'.[8] For example, in a 1900 resolution passed in Seattle by the Western Central Labor Union, Asian immigrants were vilified as 'pauper aliens' who were 'contracted for and hired for work on railways and diverse places to the detriment of American workmen'.[9] We can find repeated examples of explicit union activity calling for the racialised exclusion of workers from various workforces in parts of the British Empire, particularly in the settler colonies. For example, in 1878 the Australian Seamen's Union went on strike against the Australian Steam Navigation Company to protest its use of Chinese sailors.[10]

Certainly, formalised trade union activity could fore-close radical friendship through discriminatory practices, and by the late nineteenth century racism was thoroughly baked into assumptions about who counted as a worker deemed worthy of protection. However, looking to earlier histories of workers co-conspiracy we see how friendship and more diffuse forms of collectivity were also key to creating alternative forms of worker power. Prior to the partial legalisation of trade unions – Pitt's Combination Acts were not repealed until 1824 – early proto-union movements were forced to operate underground, and regional and trans-local coordination, informal friend-ships and other forms of short-lived collectivity were key to the development of networks of working-class struggle.

For example, in the Luddite movement. Powered by skilled workers from the Midlands and the North of England, Luddism emerged out of the harsh economic climate created by the Napoleonic Wars. The war economy meant high unemployment and inflation and prompted a rise in difficult working conditions in the new and expanding textile factories. Luddites objected primarily to the use of automated textile equipment which threatened their jobs and livelihoods. The first stirrings began in Arnold, Nottingham, on 11 March 1811 and spread rapidly throughout England over the following two years. Many Luddite groups were relatively well coordinated and used machine breaking as one of several strategies to achieve specific political goals. Along with raids, Luddites coordinated public protests and sent letters to industrialists and government officials, explaining their motives for destroying machinery and threatening further action if the use of 'obnoxious' machines persisted.[11] These workers were operating without legal unions, and they were often on the fringes of organisations that were able to offer some limited protections. In the Midlands, for example, Luddites often legitimised their demands by invoking the authority of the Company of Framework Knitters, a recognised public body that already negotiated openly with employers through designated representatives. Generally though, these workers were engaging in clandestine forms of co-conspiracy, which both relied on, and helped to construct, powerful affective bonds, albeit often short-lived.

Luddite identity was animated by loyalty to a folk-loric leader – General Ned Ludd. Ludd, so the story goes, was a weaver from Anstey, near Leicester, who, after being wronged by his boss (whipped for idleness in most accounts), smashed two new knitting frames in 1779. There is no evidence as to the veracity of the tale, but that is a moot point – real or not, Ludd helped to create a powerful diffuse movement. Importantly, Luddism 'was pan-regional, but action and physical connections were often based on the local "neighbourhood"'. Many local Luddites had 'an acute awareness of national and international events', betraying a wide knowledge of contexts far beyond their own.[12] These sorts of connections contradict the impression that Luddism was a crude movement of ill-educated protesters. Rather, 'it was not a blind reaction against economic change but a desperate adjunct of the well-informed and increasingly progressive early trade unionism'.[13]

While some of the Luddites' pan-regional networks didn't work in practice, the perception of them was key. The imaginary spectre of thousands of machine breakers, connected through clandestine friendship networks, was a crucial means through which to instil fear in their employers. Katrina Navickas describes a probable spy who 'attended a meeting of delegates in a Manchester pub, where "never was more surprised in my life when I heard the Manchester delegate lay down the plans and communications with other towns, first acting [as] if all Persons there were friends"'.[14] A Thomas Miller of Stockport was present at the meeting and reported: 'all was going on far beyond expectation that the Country Districts were pushing it from one to another as fast as possible that 900 had taken the Oath in Manchester'.[15]

Here we see that just the *idea* of friendship and solidarity created a mythology that proved generative for all sorts of working-class individuals and communities. Two decades later, agricultural workers in Southern England pursued different fleeting forms of collective direct action under the 'leadership' of another mythological figure. 'Captain Swing' was the pseudonym signed on numerous threatening letters during the 1830 Swing Riots, a wave of protests by rural labourers opposing the introduction of threshing machines, which endangered their jobs and means of survival. Captain Swing – or Rebecca if you were an agricultural worker engaged in similar forms of direct action in Wales in the early 1840s, leaving threatening notes signed 'Merched Beca' (Welsh for 'Rebecca's daughters') – became shorthand for a form of solidarity and admittance to an imagined community of similarly exploited fellow travellers. Lacking any real-life national leaders to take up their cause, workers used these imagined characters to create connection, and to ensure that geographically disparate actions and workers became linked in the public mind.

It is clear that friendship has long facilitated workers' collective struggle and forms of trade unionism, but also that the trope of friendship was often utilised to achieve particular ends. Across these histories of workers' combination and co-conspiracy we see that friendship can also be instrumentalised in service of capital. Recent trade union struggles – including the 2018–22 University College Union (UCU) industrial disputes we both participated in, as well as a range of actions from logistics to hospitality – have also had to reckon with the potential and limits of friendship in work. But what about those forms of work which require or demand forms of emotional intimacy as part of the job? And can friendship itself be a form of work?

## EMOTIONAL LABOUR

What's the going rate for a shoulder to cry on? In 2021, Twitter user Seerut K. Chawla managed to capture attention on the site for a short while with a picture of a spreadsheet and the caption: 'This is not parody. This is a real "emotional labour" invoice.' Here, acts of intimacy, care and compassion were written in a table across from a price for how much they would cost the recipient: 'endured your microagression(s) = \$200', 'taught you about microagression(s) = \$300', etc.[16] This post followed a flurry of articles about 'emotional labour', many referencing a thread on the website MetaFilter, in which hundreds of the forum's users had catalogued their resentment and disbelief at the unequal ways in which they were expected to take on the majority of caring, planning and emotional tasks in their various familial, and social, setups.[17] Though many of these responses discussed 'emotional labour' in romantic relationships, others picked up on arguments from the piece that initially galvanised the forum chats – '"Where's My Cut?": On Unpaid Emotional Labor', by writer Jess Zimmerman – which focused more on the experience of being expected to provide support and 'free therapy' for friends.[18]

As Zimmerman frames it: 'people are disturbed by the very notion that someone would charge, or pay, for friendly support. It's supposed to come free. Why?'[19] Many respondents were similarly resentful about demanding, unreciprocated and draining friendships – along with the expectation of managing their husband's and families' friendships for them. It was particularly this expansion of 'emotional labour' to the domain of friendship that rankled some commentators, including Jezebel writer Hazel Cills, who argued, 'listening to your friend talk about their bad day isn't emotional labor; it's just being a friend'.[20] Subsequent critiques focused upon other factors too: how the original formulation of emotional labour in the work of the anthropologist Arlie Hochschild had been misapplied; how these women were generally privileged (white, middle and upper class, based in the United States); and how uncomfortable the language of 'labour' felt for some, when applied to domestic experiences of love, friendship and care. Hochschild herself was called upon by *The Atlantic* to adjudicate this small explosion of everyday 'emotional labour' theorising, telling the magazine: 'There seems an alienation or a disenchantment of acts that normally we associate with the expression of connection, love, commitment. Like "Oh, what a burden it is to pick out gifts for the holiday for my children." I feel a strong need to point out that this isn't inherently an alienating act.'[21] Had the MetaFilter mums got it wrong?

A more generous reading of this strange moment – how often do we see the language of 1980s Marxist feminism breaking into mainstream contemporary discourse? – would see the women who were so animated by ideas of 'emotional labour' as engaging in a kind of consciousness raising. Clearly, most of them were doing this from a position of wealth and privilege, where 'managing' the family was often compared to running a small business, and hiring domestic 'help' was invoked as a feminist act. Gemma Hartley's opinion piece and subsequent book, *Fed Up: Emotional Labor, Women, and the Way Forward*, popularised this particular outlook, explicitly sidelining structural analysis in favour of guiding women on how to recognise, bring up and smooth over inequalities in private familial relationships.[22] This was coupled with a particular kind of 'lean in' and 'girl boss' feminism that positions domestic inequity as a barrier to individual career success, whilst ignoring structural and intersectional forms of oppression.[23] As Lola Olufemi argues, 'liberal feminism's obsession with getting women "to the top" masks a desire to ensure that the current system and its violent consequences remain intact … [rendering invisible] the work of women of color, lower paid workers and migrants who must suffer so that others may "succeed"'.[24]

And yet, however theoretically inaccurate these women were, and however much they drew on structures of racism and exclusion, in evoking the language of 'labour' to describe tasks of care or love they also gestured towards a nascent critique of work and the gendered assumptions of social reproduction. They spoke to the genuine stress and misery of maintaining 'work readiness' in increasingly 'boundaryless workplaces' where bosses (and entrepreneurial algorithms) expect constant access and attention, along with the high-expense social and leisure lives of the upper middle class, so entangled in such work. Many were just sad and tired of men who had seemed emotionally available and thoughtful in the early stages of their relationships, until this quickly evaporated and they were expected to be 'his mommy' (sometimes with the encouragement or tutelage of their partner's actual mum). In rejecting having to 'mother' their husbands and friends, these women reinscribe a certain 'pure' kernel of mothering (presumably in an individuated relation with *their* children alone), but also point to having lost any sense of their own social and emotional lives beyond them being instrumentalised for work and family. They also expose how, even for the privileged middle classes, certain types of activity are deemed 'productive' or valuable to capitalism, and others are not, despite how vital they may be to sustaining life. These acts might not be 'inherently alienating', to return to Hochschild, yet people certainly seem alienated. But are they?

Hochschild coined the idea of 'emotional labour' in her 1983 book, *The Managed Heart*, an ethnographic study of how airline hostesses and bailiffs manage and shape their emotional states as part of their work.[25] Her argument draws on Marxist theories of the commodity form and alienation to explain how workers manage their feelings 'to create a publicly observable facial and bodily display'.[26] For instance, smiling, comforting and soothing airline passengers during a flight. Hochschild distinguishes between this process in the 'private sphere' of our lives, which she calls 'emotion work', and the 'transmutation' of such feelings into the 'public sphere' of work, where they become a commodified emotional experience that bosses promise and customers expect. This is 'emotional labour', and like physical or mental labour in Marxist scholarship, it entails alienation or disconnect from the products and conditions of one's labour, in that such 'transmutation' results in personal, private feelings being moulded and controlled until they end up belonging more 'to the organization and less to the self'.[27] This is compounded by the fact that workers' emotional states must be subordinated through such interactions – 'the customer is always right' – and in the imposition of managerial 'feeling rules' that bosses create to determine how, when and what kind of emotional displays are required of workers. Hochschild also argues that such rules go beyond mere compliance, which she frames as 'surface acting', and instead encourage workers to engage in a kind of 'deep acting' where they internalise the feelings and emotional displays stipulated by management.[28] Such 'fusions' of the real and acted self may allow one to excel at work, but for Hochschild they entail a dangerous suppression and alienation of the individual self.

Hochschild connects her 'private'/'public' distinction to the notions of 'use value' and 'exchange value' in Marx, stating that emotional labour 'is sold for a wage and therefore has exchange value', and instead using the 'synonymous terms emotion work or emotion management to refer to those same acts done in a private context where they have *use* value'.[29] Emotional work is only emotional labour when it has the capacity to be sold as a form of labour power. As the sociologist Paul Brook argues:

> In applying Marx's concept of wage-labour, Hochschild makes the crucial distinction between labour and labour power. Thus, the worker sells their labour power (as the yet-to-be realized capacity to work) rather than their completed labour in the form of a product ... For Marx, this distinction is to indicate that a worker's physical and mental (and by implication emotional) capabilities exist in an ongoing, uncertain relationship to their employer ... This is because labour power is unlike all

other commodities, owing to employers being unable to control completely its final form or cost as a consequence of their inability to detach it physically, mentally or emotionally from the individual worker.[30]

This uncertainty can allow for resistance and non-compliance, even the withdrawal of emotional labour or collective organising around this. In contrast to the 1970s 'Wages for Housework' movement, which aimed to expose capitalism's reliance on unpaid reproductive labour through a demand that it be valued,[31] Hochschild simply delineates a particular *type* of labour that was under-theorised in Marx's schema. She sees emotional labour as an aspect, like mental and physical labour, of most if not all work, but shows its particular importance in the kinds of service work that have rapidly expanded since *The Managed Heart* was published.

Crucially, a substantial amount of this expansion has involved the encroachment of work into what had historically been the 'private' and domestic sphere of social reproduction. Hochschild's distinctions between 'private'/'public', 'use'/'exchange' and 'emotional work'/'emotional labour' pivot on the capacity for an activity to be deemed 'productive', to be offered as a commodity of labour power on the market. Relatedly, an orthodox Marxist conception of alienation – the agency-removing separation of a worker from the products and conditions of their labour – occurs only through 'productive' work. But when production and reproduction feel so blurred, do we really have to be paid (or have the possibility to be paid) to be alienated? And how, in analysing the differences between what is and what is not deemed 'productive' in our current economic system, do we avoid reproducing judgements about 'unproductive' work as somehow less important terrain for political struggle? Even Hochschild seems unsure about this, moving in the aforementioned *Atlantic* interview from defining emotional labour as 'the work, for which you're paid, which centrally involves trying to feel the right feeling for the job', to this newer usage of the term: 'I do think that managing anxiety associated with obligatory chores is emotional labor.'[32]

For the MetaFilter users, the issue is not just confusing private 'emotion work' with public 'emotional labour', it's that so many more of these 'private' acts of care and love *do* have commodified forms in contemporary capitalism, and they resent the expectation they will perform these without recognition or renumeration. In fact, in managing the small industries of nannies, au pairs, therapists, tutors and communication gadgets that people assume to be required in this strata of society, such women know very well the price of such work, and feel it to be beneath them. On the original thread, one commenter – who goes on to document divorcing her husband and quitting her job after taking part in the discussion – puts it as such:

> Where I live, the entire economy depends on exploiting minority ethnicity [*sic*] women to handle the third shift of the middle and upper class, and increasingly even the working class. I pay twice the going rate for my household help so she gets a fair wage, decent working hours with weekends and public holidays off, and as a result,

I'm being judged against parents with live-in round the clock nannies.

In a strange way then, there is a kind of alienation going on here, the imagined alienation of the (racialised, migrant and otherwise marginalised) care worker by people who buy this labour power rather than sell it. There's also what we might call 'reproductive alienation': an estrangement from acts of care due to the blurriness of how such acts sit within capitalism, from struggling to delineate economic 'value' at the edges of 'productivity'. This works in tandem with a sense of stress and resentment about acts that people find harder to outsource or fit into their lives, things like sex, choosing birthday presents or, of course, acts of friendship. For while friendship usually involves a whole lot of 'emotion work', it's harder to imagine how this might take the form of exchange value, or a kind of labour power that can be bought and sold. Or is it?

## WOOING THE ALGORITHM

Joel goes for lunch with a friend who is visiting. She's worked for years in theatre in England, but has been struggling to pay the bills as cuts to the arts have meant an increasingly stark lack of opportunities. A talented illustrator and artist, she started doing tattoos for friends to earn a bit of extra money. After a year or so, with funded arts and theatre 'more fucked than ever', as she put it, she'd decided to try make a go of the tattooing in a more serious way. As she explained:

A friend who's been doing this kind of work for a while sat me down and explained how they approach it, how to build that online presence on Instagram and stuff. I hate doing social media really but it's so necessary if I want to actually get paid beyond tattooing pals at 'mates rates', though this was really useful in terms of getting practice and building a portfolio. Anyway, this friend reads up on all the social media algorithms and how to cut through online, she's kind of obsessed. She said firstly, I have to log on everyday and make new content. I have to put my face in the pictures and stories, and ask questions or use bits of short text that hook people in.

The key next thing is to not imagine a particular customer but to instead pitch yourself to the algorithm, imagine your wooing the algorithm! And then the algorithm sends it out. And the main thing with tattoos, when you're sitting for that long with someone, is that people want to think of you as a friend. You need to communicate this through social media, give them a bit of yourself. And they want to know 'the person behind the art' or whatever. So now, even though I hate it really, I log in every day and I try and make these potential clients feel like they know me, like I'm their friend. I just treat it as work, an hour a day doing my online content. And it works! It's helping pay the bills for the first time, but I do feel strange having to put myself out there like that.

Here was a person used to the networking and hustle of arts work in Britain, where 'personal brands', nepotism and unpaid (and therefore exclusionary) work are important factors in gaining and sustaining paid employment. Yet something felt different in the shift to self-employed tattooing and the online marketing of this. Friendship was no longer just a route *to* work, or something you might experience *in* work: friendship was the work. For while the skills and artistry of a particular tattooist may be key for people in choosing their next tattoo, this is transformed and mediated by the ways in which they can feel a closeness to, a shared sense of interests with, and generally 'get to know' the person tattooing them, mainly through consuming their daily social media activity. Such work involves various forms and expressions of emotional labour, but unlike the codified and uniform 'feeling rules' of, say, air hostessing or generalised service work, the emphasis here is on the uniqueness and authenticity of both the work and the worker. Crucially, this is mediated by online platforms that have become indispensable for a wide range of workers – artists, journalists, small businesses, childcarers, sex workers, to name a few – and that explicitly reward and distribute performances of authenticity and intimacy. Both 'producers' and 'clients' create profits and valuable data for such platforms by interacting through them, and across the range of algorithmic and technological strategies employed by such platforms a key focus persists: keep people online.

This broader tendency is what we framed in our Introduction as 'ambient friendship': the saturated forms of constant connectivity without connection that are intrinsic to social media. 'Ambient friendship' works to keep us logged on and available, and to blur the lines between friendship and work. Just as the proliferation of ambient

'music to work to' playlists reflects the incessant, streaming productivity of the Spotify offices that create them,
platforms such as Facebook and Twitter reflect the
'friendship as constant networking' ethos of their Silicon
Valley creators. That increasing numbers of us use these
platforms in ways that meld our work and social lives
is built into such platforms by design. Though most of
us don't have access to the lunchtime ping-pong tables
and free Kombucha of a Google-style office, we do live
in the online world that originates from the work ethic
and instrumental view of social life created within these
spaces. Sociality is reduced to boosting productivity
and offering new sources of revenue. The blurriness of
online interaction, and the ways in which both individual attempts at monetisation and the wider profit-motive
of the platforms themselves are hidden behind a veneer of
'connection', work to increase our overall screen-time. For
those who've committed to social media work as a main
source of income, discerning 'grift' from 'real connection' often involves a questioning of the self: how to draw
the line between my personhood and personal brand? In
her research on Czech social media influencers, Marie
Heřmanová notes how many of them would communicate a desire for 'sharing something without revealing too
much'. This meant balancing a sense of personal privacy
with the need to establish 'a certain level of intimacy with
their followers to stay authentic and relatable', all whilst
attempting to guide followers' consumption patterns.[33]
Here we can see how, even for tattooing, an artform where
the relationship between artist, art and client couldn't be
more intimately connected (talk about personal brand-

ing!), people can still feel alienated from work that they must 'give a bit of themselves' to everyday.

To 'woo' an algorithm is to cultivate a version of the self that encourages people to spend more time on the platform, through encouraging them to engage with an element within it: 'you'. While private and direct messages within such platforms might feel less exposed, these still ultimately guide how different algorithms judge 'user interaction' and closeness between users. From Instagram to Twitter, all interactions, from 'sliding into DMs' to liking a celebrity dance craze, are then collected as data and metadata that informs future algorithms and is highly valuable to advertisers. Even in 'encrypted' services such as WhatsApp, which was bought by Facebook for $19.6 billion in 2014, such metadata – often compared to the 'envelope' of who sent and received what, and when and where they did so, in contrast with the actual 'contents' of the letter – is captured and monetised in such a way.[34] Clearly, social interaction is extremely valuable, even in (currently) 'ad-free' platforms like WhatsApp. The global scale and growth of the messaging service, its ubiquity and necessity for social life in many places, has made it a key part of Mark Zuckerberg's 'Meta', the conglomerate parent company he built from Facebook, taking in Instagram, Threads and others. Zuckerberg said as much himself in 2023, in a *New York Times* interview about his plans to start monetising WhatsApp: 'Now that everyone has mobile phones and are basically producing content and messaging all day long, I think you can do something that's a lot better and more intimate than just a feed of all your friends.'[35] This vision, of a constant stream of 'interaction-as-content', shapes how anyone on such platforms does friendship, even if they resist it. Over the years – as we come to think of friendship groups by their WhatsApp group names, or parse our different friends and family across different profiles and apps – it influences how we understand and define friendship itself. The blur between work and leisure, between production and reproduction, feels all the more acute within such a context. Even for the most assiduous gatekeeper of separate profiles and online spaces, the boss and the best friend are always threatening to jostle into the same screen. The capture and enclosure of friendship within such platforms can be hard to differentiate from more purely instrumental productions of 'friending', even when they do still hold space for all kinds of real and intimate connection. Ultimately, friendship on such platforms can often feel like work, and for certain groups of so-called cultural and knowledge workers, it increasingly is.

The platforms where many of us now do friendship involve invisibilised exploitation in a more traditional sense. Platform capitalism relies on all kinds of underpaid labour. Union drives within tech firms, and attempts at union-busting to stop this, have mushroomed in the last decade, often driven by the most exploited workers. At Meta, it is the subcontracted cleaning, maintenance, security and food staff who have been at the forefront. Cleaners at Facebook's London HQ on Brock Street protested in 2021, after their duties were doubled without an increase in staff or pay. Miriam Palencia, 42, told *The Guardian*: 'A manager threatened me with a sanction if I didn't clean one-and-a-half floors. He timed how long I took. It was hell. I had a haemorrhage on one of my shifts because of the stress.'[36] Moderation responsibilities are also often outsourced by such firms, the very functioning of the algorithm depending on teams of low-paid workers filtering reems of private data at speed. A ProPublica investigation into WhatsApp describes how 'more than 1,000 contract workers filling floors of office buildings in Austin, Texas, Dublin and Singapore' are paid around $16.50 an hour to 'sift through millions of private messages, images and videos. They pass judgment on whatever flashes on their screen – claims of everything from fraud or spam to child porn and potential terrorist plotting – typically in less than a minute.'[37] Kenya-based outsourcing company Sama – which markets itself as 'lifting people out of poverty' by getting them £7 a day AI-training and data moderation jobs – is one of many that publicly stepped back from Meta moderation work in 2023 due to the traumatising effect on employees. The functioning of social media platforms relies on a whole range of similarly exploitative material foundations. Capital's expansion into social life, and the particular blurs of work/non-work that come with this, is scaffolded by a stratum of underpaid workers that the platform attempts to render invisible. Contemporary friendship, in practice and as an idea, emerges in part from these platforms. Any attempt to reconfigure this, and to improve conditions for the 'cultural' and 'knowledge' workers who rely on the platform, must involve linking with struggles amongst the most exploited workers who underpin them.

In broader terms, 'emotional labour', and new forms of what we might call 'friendship labour', are similarly embedded in wider economic structures. As Paul Brook argues in a 'critical defence' of emotional labour:

> All service production, whether in shops, airlines, call centres, hospitals or schools, depends upon a myriad of other fixed capital, technical and support work inputs in addition to the emotional performance (principally, buildings, technical equipment, 'back-office' support and codified 'feeling rules'). Moreover, politico-economic forces such as market competition, labour market conditions, new technologies and public services marketization also exercise considerable influence on the structure, design and standards of service labour processes.[38]

How and when emotional work becomes a kind of labour power, and who is able monetise their intimate life and friendships, depends on such wider factors. This is deeply gendered and racialised, as well as unevenly distributed globally. Many of the authors of 'emotional labour' blogs and commentaries that we opened with fall short in failing to consider this wider structural context. They also miss how acts of befriending, caring and physical or emotional intimacy have a long history as paid work, and overlook writing by Black feminists, sex workers and others on this topic.[39] In her original piece Zimmerman jokily considers advertising 'friend services' on Etsy, before ultimately deciding that imagined remuneration is enough: 'I don't expect to get anything, really. But at least now I know that when I get nothing, I'm being cheated.' The power of being able to shock through naming possible prices for acts that are assumed to be outside of market relations ultimately relies upon the same binaries it purports to challenge: unpaid/paid, reproductive/productive. Unlike more structurally critical writing on such topics, Zimmerman is here not interested in wider issues such as poverty, criminalisation, access to housing, living costs and racism (beyond a passing remark that white women should also 'recompense' women of colour in an analogous way to the '#GiveYourMoneyToWomen' hashtag she endorses), all of which constitute how care is distributed under capitalism. The problem is not that redistributing some cash around is antithetical to 'real' friendship, but that this would do little to address the underlying structures that make voluntary redistribution seem like a radical option.

## GONE TO BRUNCH!

Social media platforms are key to how contemporary sociality is used to boost worker productivity, both within work and through shaping reproductive leisure activities outside the workplace. They also encourage people to monetise social life in ways that blur distinctions between work and non-work, whilst entrenching a wider work ethic. Leisure activities and venues themselves become geared towards online reproduction and virality: many restaurants now use Instagram-able gimmicks like glitter-salt and dry-ice clouds to present food, or have photo booths and QR codes for review and engagement embedded into the furniture. Such spaces are 'ambient friendship' made material, embedding the ethics of the platform in physical space: 'connection-as-content', constant streaming, and forms of emotional labour that go beyond a clear 'service' interaction. Similarly, venues for everything from indoor mini-golf to axe-throwing and novelty darts construe 'leisure' primarily through the prism of the 'work night out' or 'corporate away day'. Public sociality becomes an often expensive and constantly 'novel' mirror to work. The archetypal leisure space here is always 'pop-up', emerging for short hype-filled windows in different spaces, rather than rooted in or attempting to build community. So-called 'high culture' leisure spaces like theatres and concert halls – whilst continuing to perform their older functions as networking and conspicuous consumption venues – increasingly integrate similar social media informed approaches into their programming. Across the board, workers in the leisure industries juggle bad pay, emotional labour demands and a lack of access to leisure time themselves.

Like platform capitalism, the leisure industries in privileged parts of Europe and North America rely on a whole layer of underpaid staff, along with deeply exploitative global supply chains. As the authors of the Zine *Abolish Restaurants* argue:

Although everything in the restaurant is put into motion and works only because we make it work, the restaurant is something outside and against us. The harder we work, the more money the restaurant makes. The less we are paid, the more money the restaurant makes. It is rare that the workers in a restaurant can afford to eat regularly at the restaurant they work in. It is common for restaurant workers to carry plates of exquisite food around all night, while having nothing but coffee and bread in our stomachs.[40]

Pointing this out, in an era where many people feel continually confused and guilty about their own power as consumers ('ethical' or otherwise), is neither fashionable nor particularly fun ('who invited these guys to the party?'). But beyond arguments about personal consumptive responsibility, understanding the structural ways in which our friendships and social lives are moulded by such frameworks is important to imagining something different. In *BFFs: The Radical Potential of Female Friendship*, writer Anahit Behrooz contrasts two types of friendship, informed by a similar critique of 'leisure':

> My friend sent me a TikTok some time ago, which – if I scroll through our messages – seems to constitute half our textual language. In it, a young person discusses alternative forms of spending time with friends that don't rely on spending money on coffees and lunches and trips away, that instead embed friendship in the quotidian rhythm of life. They use a framework that is new to me, radical in its tender mundanity: friends you might go on errands with. These are the friendships where quality time is constructed not through the luxurious artifice of time spent away from the responsibilities of life, but through the collective experience of these responsibilities, where doing the weekly grocery shop and filing taxes and working out are as much, and indeed more, an opportunity for intimacy as a mandated, bookended slot of leisure time.

I had never heard of the errand friend ... But for a long time now, I have felt a resentment for the opposite of the errand friend: the kind of friendship that seems only to take place on occasions, that is lifted out of the everyday. I have, in my mind, dubbed this the brunch friendship; although this isn't particularly original or, indeed, fair – maybe it isn't kind to be petulant about others' joys. Yet, something about the idea of brunch – not the meal but the concept, the social structure, the exaggerated performance of middle-class femininity that it represents – sets me on edge. Perhaps it is its rigidity that feels emotionally impoverished, that undoes the queered, throwaway softness of the errand friend; the bulk of a table suddenly between two people, everything clothed in politeness and a synthetic glitz. It has come to signify everything I fear about how the friendships in my life might go: a bimonthly catch-up in a depersonalised space, the death rattle of what were once entangled lives, now pulled apart and frayed.[41]

Some relationships are more brunch than friend. To build on Behrooz's argument further, perhaps 'brunch' not only illuminates a disentanglement, but actively contributes to this, by instead enmeshing people in the particular moulds of 'ambient friendship' we've been analysing so far. The 'brunch friend' is highly amenable to social media. They might be struggling with feeling both isolated and socially saturated, attempting to fit people into a social calendar that blurs with their work calendar. Brunch dates may have the timbre of a work meeting, and often overlap with these. Brunch is a place where these very blurs are played out and investigated: where gossip, networking, pitching for jobs, 'checking in' and oversharing become hard to differentiate, and seem very different to the rhythms of everyday connection we might once have had.

Questions of 'brunch' might also convey a political quality to some readers, linked to the derision of 'brunch democrats' in US politics. The phrase originates from a protest placard from a 2019 Women's March that infamously declared, 'If Hillary was president, we'd all be at brunch.'[42] This sentiment seemed to encapsulate a white middle-class and centrist indifference to the hardships and difficulties facing many people, beyond the shock of a Trump presidency, along with a kind of entitlement to leisure-over-politics. The 'brunch friend', then, doesn't just help us summarise a particular form of platform-mandated contemporary friendship, it also speaks to the way ideas of leisure and sociality are often presented as outside, or actively escaping, politics. This particular kind of brunch signifies a form of anti-political friendship. It turns friendship into something that soothes the worst aspects of work and familial reproduction, whilst infusing a busy 'productivity' and consumptive conspicuousness into everyday life. Unsurprisingly, brunch is where the 'emotional labour' MetaFilter posters often seem to thrash out their annoyance and confusion at their roles within such systems of extraction, coming to anti-political, individualised conclusions.

Frustrations with leisure-heavy friendship, and a desire for the 'tender mundanity' that Behrooz highlights, also point to ways in which friendship itself can feel like work, particularly for people who find the pressures of social interaction challenging. Enforced sociality and lengthy social engagements can sometimes feel tiresome, and even more so for neurodivergent people. Instead, radical friendship might look like companionable silence, parallel play, or alone togetherness. A friend of Laura's is part of a queer gardening group (Top Soil!) and finds some of their most nourishing friendships there, despite not always staying very long or engaging in much conversation. They describe the feeling of doing something – repotting a Geranium or harvesting peas – next to someone else weeding the same bed. Doing these things together, caring collectively, feeling connected, without feeling the pressure of making plans, 'catching-up', or even having to make eye contact, can be a valuable way of subverting the consumptive conspicuousness of much capitalist sociality, and can also just feel really good!

With the same green-fingered friend Laura recently inaugurated fortnightly Dad beers at the local pub. Dad beers is an attempt to replicate the Thursday pints that Laura's Dad and his mate had as a regular fixture for years. The arrangement was simple – every Thursday they met at the local pub at 10 pm, had two pints – sometimes talking a lot, other times not so much – before kick out time at 11.30 pm. The stereotype of men standing at the bar, together but separate, drinking pints looking ahead rather than face to face, might conjure an image of lonely masculinity, but for us we have found in it a warm companionship, a calm assuredness in friendship that is the antithesis of the pressure of performative brunching. For Laura's Dad, Dad beers was a regular fixture, with no need for coordinating or planning, and contact was only made beforehand if one *couldn't* make the date. Again, there is something wonderfully mundane and low stakes here – a casual but determined effort to avoid the constant back and forth of endless 'when are you free?'s and complex diary coordination.

\* \* \*

Work conditions most of our lives in profound ways. It is no surprise then that many of our friendships are refracted through work. In this chapter we have attempted to overview some of these links, with a focus on the ways that distinctions between work/non-work and 'productivity' inform how people practise and narrate their social lives. Early histories of combination and trade unionism showed the enmeshment of social ties within work, along with the potential for this to reinforce forms of exclusion and racism. Despite this, friendship – both real and collectively imagined – was key to the interconnected forms of militancy practised by many in resisting capitalist capture and enclosure. Such histories percolate into the contemporary ways in which people are able (or unable) to divide their social, reproductive and working lives, with recent interest in 'emotional labour' signalling an upper-middle-class attempt to reconsider such boundaries. Missing from such discourse around this is a deeper analysis of the wider systems of racialised exploitation and technological capture that facilitate contemporary friendship and leisure, along with what is lost for everyone when 'ambient friendship' takes hold. Behrooz's evocative distinction between the 'brunch' and 'errand' friend takes us full circle in some ways, back to shared activity and coexistence, the kinds of accompaniment and fraternity we sketched in the last chapter.

Of course, joint errands and Dad beers are just first steps towards more radically transformative kinds of mutual struggle. What kinds of 'errands' might we share in service of anti-capitalist social reproduction, of generating 'dense bonds' and revolutionary strategy? What might it mean to imagine our relationships in a world beyond work? And to build an anti-work ethos into our approach to friendship? In the next chapter we look at ways that people have pursued friendship beyond the immediate conditions in which they find themselves, as part of efforts to make links between people living in different places and in different ways. In doing so we ask: is friendship capable of challenging settled ideas and old prejudices? We think so, and next we will see how this has often been most potently felt on the move.

# Conversation with Gracie Mae Bradley

In the winter of 2023, we asked our friend Gracie Mae Bradley – co-author of *Against Borders: The Case for Abolition* and founding member of the Against Borders for Children (ABC) campaign – about how friendship figures in her life. As a writer-campaigner, Bradley is often on the move, her work very much intertwined with people and movements in various parts of the world. Our conversation was prompted by Gracie's blog post 'On Hospitality'.[1] In it she describes travelling to record an episode of the Border Abolitionist 'De Verbranders' podcast in Amsterdam and to the Feminist Autonomous Research Centre's No Borders Summer School in Athens through the early part of summer 2023.[2] As Gracie put it:

> [This was] the first extended time since [the Covid lockdown] that I've spent wandering around intermittently with other people, rather than on my own or with my partner. So I'm remembering how it feels to catch an evening on the wing of a gentle invitation; to follow a kind stranger's recommendations through a city's hot night.

She goes on to describe the Summer School:

> There were whole rooms and faces from Delhi, Lisbon, Palermo and beyond at the opening assembly ... we

spoke with one another about what the border is doing to people where each of us lives, how burned out and tired many people resisting the violence are; how degrading the conditions in the camps are; and the inadequacy of some of our movement spaces at meaningfully dealing with harm. Only that day we had learned that hundreds of people had died in a shipwreck at Pylos, many of them shut in the hold of a rusting trawler. There is no solace for deaths that should not have occurred, so that isn't the world that I want: I am thinking of what it was to feel our anger and sorrow together, to be able to hold one another's hands and regulate our breaths in the same room and air, rather than alone and behind a screen.

It isn't only in my recent travels that I have been thinking about how hospitality shows itself. I now live much further away from some of my old friends, and our time together, shorter though it is, has a different timbre and intensity, because it stretches over days. Between the voicenotes and text dumps we're back in the teenage intimacy of long weekends in one another's homes, camped out on sofas, long breakfasts, jumping in one another's beds in the mornings.

… All of which is to say that when we were all separated from one another I missed this, and I am grateful to be reminded of what can happen when we let our guard down, when we decide to pitch up somewhere, and meet open arms. And I am grateful that my own life is such that my door is a place at which friends can pitch up hot and tired and know welcome. You know, insert something profound and not too subtle here on all of this being the antithesis of bordering; on the importance of giving centre stage to what and whom we love.

**Joel**: I loved reading that blog post! You really capture something about friendship, and the importance of unstructured time with friends. With the realities of work, though, this often feels difficult – how do you keep space for this sort of friendship?

**Gracie**: I suppose the thing for me is that one of the many realities of life under racial capitalism is that unless you're independently wealthy, you're working, and you're spending a lot of your waking time doing paid work. And while this can't be collapsed into the kinds of work that many people do that is actively degrading or dangerous, and those contexts in which labour rights are routinely denied, many of us are still operating in institutional contexts that are not super welcoming, or might be hostile to us, or just, not in alignment with our values. And so we spend a lot of our waking time in these potentially quite unfriendly environments, so spaces where we get to spend time with fellow travellers, I think, are really important. They're important reminders of what we can be to each other. [In Athens, at the Feminist No Borders Summer School] I was in the company of fellow travellers. And I guess when I say fellow travellers, I don't mean that we agree with each other on absolutely everything. We have an investment in a shared project, that is border abolition, abolition feminism, and I think investment in shared projects, it lets me let my guard down. It lets me trust people. And it means that when we agree, but crucially when we disagree, our starting point is very different to where we start when we disagree with people with whom we have no common cause.

I think that the influence of these trips and encounters on my political work has been really significant in terms of just like, helping me to keep the faith. To actually just keep believing that this world that we talk about, and that we talk about making together, is possible, because we prefigure it. It's a reminder that what we write about and what we write towards, these aren't kind of ideals that are off in the distance. These are things that can happen for us, that we can make together, even in the world that we live in now. It's restorative.

**Joel**: Totally. I'm interested though, in connecting this to how much of a role you think friendship should play in more formal kinds of political organising? Where's the line for you?

**Gracie**: I find this question interesting and challenging, because as I said earlier, there's an inherent trust to friendship. So, it can be easy to do political work with your friends because there's a shared basis of trust. If you've helped to put someone's kids to bed or you've been in their home, there's a trust that's there. That means that you can do risky stuff together. But you can also do vulnerable stuff together, and world making is a vulnerable thing, to open yourself up and say, 'I would really like the world to be this way', that's vulnerable. I think sometimes political work requires friendship. And sometimes it inculcates friendship.

But in terms of the limit, there are a lot of black feminist thinkers and organisers who've written about the importance of *coalition* organising, in order to get to where we want to politically, and they've also written about the fact that a coalition isn't home … you've got to be able to organise with people with whom you disagree, people who hold beliefs that we find challenging, and also just people who we find annoying, who rub us up the wrong way. I obviously don't mean organising with people who want me or my family – or anyone else for that matter – dead, but there are still a lot of people who we disagree with who might find it useful to work with at times. And it's not just about doing political work with people that we're not friends with, it's also about doing political work *for* or in solidarity with people that we're not actually that keen on. I don't have to be someone's friend to believe that they're worthy of all the things that a person needs to live a flourishing life. And I think that that is a really, really important line to draw.

I have certainly seen a fair amount of political organising feeling like a scene or an in group. And seen it be hard for people to get involved. An over reliance on informal friendship networks and relations of trust can mean that you don't develop the structures that allow you to welcome and bring people in who just are completely random and don't know anyone at all. So I think it's quite double edged. But there's also a frivolity to friendship – I mean, not that all political organising has to be really serious – but just I guess there's something to do with obligation in political organising. And there's a lot that we do with our friends that has nothing to do with obligation at all. And it's really important that we have that too.

# CHAPTER THREE

# Friends of Friends

## FRIENDSHIP ON THE MOVE

This chapter argues that radical friendship is palpable –
it is *felt*, it makes ripples, it has an atmosphere, and it is
often on the move. Radical movements have forever been
charged with being naive, ineffectual, impracticable. And
yet they have created and continue to create revolutions
in everyday life and to expand human freedoms in the
here and now, not only in a utopian future. Friendship is
vital in this. This is not to say, as Gracie made clear, that
friendship always means easy company, harmonious decision making, and good times guaranteed. Far from it. But
rather that the *practice* of friendship in radical struggle –
the difficult and frustrating process of pursuing dialogue
and seeking common ground, even with people that wind
us up – is where the ideas come from! Friendship itself is
a prefigurative politic – it can embody the collaborative
world we seek to create.

The generative potential of friendship, as this book
argues, has been at the heart of revolutionary movements
in innumerable ways, but it is perhaps often most potently
charged when encountered on the move. It is on the road
that we see how friendship, intimacy, love and care experienced by those in service or pursuit of transformative

politics and alternative futures constitutes, as Gracie put it, 'the antithesis of bordering'![1]

Revolutionary movements have always relied on precisely that: movement. This chapter looks to histories of travelling activists in nineteenth-century Europe and argues that these activists relied on networks of friends of friends as a way to access hospitality, safety and solidarity on the road. And while the content of radical lectures was important in spreading radical ideas, perhaps more importantly their occurrence demanded forms of hospitality that created politically generative encounters in living rooms, in pubs, and in transit. These intimate encounters became an essential means through which an *embodied* understanding of collectivist ideas spread around Europe. We then turn to the 1990s–2000s DIY punk scene in Britain to show again how networks of friends of friends and Zine culture have been vital in forming and sustaining politically radical spaces, and also how embodied experiences of solidarity and friendship, often through music, create strong bonds. Such circuits were linked to emerging kinds of queer, ecological, No Borders and anti-racist struggle that persisted beyond the turn away from 'summit hopping' in the aftermath of the anti-globalisation movement.

## THE LECTURE TOUR

In the nineteenth century, public lectures, and the popularity (or not) of the activists who travelled to deliver them, were the yardstick by which just about any radical cause measured its reach and success. The lecture tour was a common feature of Victorian activist life for those espousing all manner of oppositional political ideas, and these tours have been much studied for the content of the lectures and the performative and oratorical style of their speakers. However, the tours were politically generative for radical and socialist communities not simply via the lectures themselves, but through the intimacies and friendships that sustained them, and that they in turn stimulated. Lecture tours saw activists on the road for weeks, months and even years at a time, often staying with workers and families in towns across Britain and beyond.

These tours happened across varying scales – regional, national and international – and activists relied on the power of friends of friends as a means through which to access networks of hospitality and find places to stay. Time and again speakers remarked that their backstage encounters were often more politically inspiring than what took place on the official platform, for both audience and speaker. It was often the friendly (or sometimes decidedly unfriendly) and informal connections that happened around the main event that proved the most politically salient. Through these more intimate encounters, the 'platform' was expanded immeasurably, as all manner of sites and relationships created new arenas for political evangelisation and revolutionary idea-swapping.

In 1837, following an extensive lecture tour around Britain, the prolific anti-slavery orator George Thompson declared: 'I have been able, by rapid movement ... and the co-operation of local friends – to diffuse throughout the country a vast amount of information.'[2] Movement, friendship and the diffusion of ideas were at the heart of revolutionary politics in this period. Activists advocating for Owenism, cooperativism, the abolition of slavery, Chartism, anti-imperialism, socialism, anarchism, Irish Independence and many others besides all relied on itinerant lecturers to carry their messages out into the hills and highways of Britain and beyond.

Some of this movement was formalised: the practice of artisans 'tramping' for work across Britain was institutionalised via trade societies and could be an important facet of labour organising;[3] and when lecturers were employed by reform groups with wealthy patrons, their tours were paid for in advance and their journeys carefully structured. However, for fledging radical organisations and oppositional groups subject to stringent policing, it was grassroots forms of political hospitality, networks of friendship and local associational structures that sustained itinerant lecturers and built movements. These grassroots friendship structures became increasingly important for anarchist lecturers in the 1890s (especially after 1896, when anarchists were expelled from the Second International) as the movement became isolated from socialist organisations at both national and international levels.

Speakers with less money behind them had to organise parts of their itinerary on the move, seeking suitable premises and raising an audience by distributing handbills and engaging the local bell ringer. In search of friends of friends in the 1840s, Chartist agents and Owenite missionaries would often enquire after radical booksellers, a list of whose names the editors of radical newspapers such as the Chartist *Northern Star* were careful to print and keep updated. By seeking out hubs of connected activists, via the bookseller for example, these radical lecturers hoped to find a friend in common and a bed for the night. In doing so, they were able to connect hyper-localised activities happening across the country, create a greater sense of fellowship, and thereby embody the politics they preached. This process could also be scaled up to connect with activists engaged in liberatory political projects elsewhere across the globe.

## REVOLUTION AROUND THE BREAKFAST TABLE

Economists describe the major expansion of trade and finance between 1870 and 1914 as the 'first globalisation'. Constance Bantman highlights a dual globalisation during this period – one state-led and capitalist, the other 'anti-hegemonic'.[4] In other words, just as capitalism became increasingly globalised, so too did anti-capitalist activism. This was an era of revolutionary globalisation, and one increasingly characterised by movement. As socialist and anarchist travelling itineraries became more ambitious (and necessary, due to the expulsion of activists from various European countries), personal interaction, domestic encounters, and practices of friendship continued to be as important as official meetings and engagements. A coherent and fully agreed upon socialist programme never emerged in Britain in this period – the movement was disparate and subject to fierce internal debates and splits, particularly around the question of parliamentary strategies. But whether or not mobile forms of messaging were key to the doctrinal coherence of the socialist movement, travelling activists were absolutely key in *making* socialists. Hospitality, intimacy and transitory connections made on the road proved to be hugely important in persuading ordinary people to the cause of socialism. Lecturers were both an embodiment and a prefiguration of a utopian politics to come.

For example, Annie Besant (made famous for her role in the London match girls' strike of 1888) recalled the political vitality of discussions that took place in the homes of local workers when she undertook a socialist lecture tour of the North East in 1878:

> In Northumberland and Durham; the miners there are, as a rule, shrewd and hard-headed men ... At Seghill and at Bedlington I have slept in their cottages and have been welcomed to their tables ... one evening at Seghill, after a lecture, when my host, himself a miner, invited about a dozen of his comrades to supper to meet me, the talk ran on politics, and I soon found that my companions knew more of English politics, had a far shrewder notion of political methods, and were, therefore, much better worth talking to than most.[5]

This is a common trope – an account of how spaces of encounter, outside of the official platform, were where some of the most generative discussions took place. Later, Agnes Henry, an Irish-born anarchist and friend of Augustin Hamon and Errico Malatesta, similarly recognised the usefulness of domestic settings in promoting revolutionary ideas. Henry lived for a time in an experimental communal house at 29 Doughty Street in Bloomsbury in the early 1890s. The house played host to numerous European socialist, anarchist and utopian activists passing through London, and Henry seems to have irritated a number of its inhabitants, particularly Edith Lees (who later married the sexologist Henry Havelock Ellis), by insisting on 'discussing Anarchist theory at the breakfast table!'[6]

Henry very much understood the political vitality that was possible only when travelling activists were able to meet, speak, eat and share intimacies in person. She was a prolific speaker and teacher. She lectured around Britain, France and Italy and lived variously in Paris, Brittany and Trinidad before returning to London to help run the Anarchist International School for children of political refugees, which the exile of the Paris Commune Louise Michel had set up at 19 Fitzroy Square in 1890. Henry was emblematic of the mobile anarchist of the period, and she consistently emphasised the importance of movement. In 1893 she wrote in *Freedom* that 'In Norwich our comrades have suffered much privation ... Still, they struggle on with a steady sort of man to man propaganda ... with occasional visits from speakers from other parts, they would be able to keep up active work.'[7]

What Henry recognised was that without able speakers, and without real-life interaction, movements could not grow. Travelling lecturers were therefore central to the flourishing of revolutionary agitation. In the pursuit of friendship and revolution, they bridged the gaps between branch, district, regional, national and international organisational structures, both formal and informal. As the Chartist leader Feargus O'Connor had said decades earlier, these mobile activists were links in a 'great chain' that connected city to city and region to region.[8]

## ROUTES OF FRIENDSHIP

Friendship also helps to explain how and where important centres of radical activity sprung up. In 1893 Agnes Henry toured North East England delivering lectures on anarchism in relation to state socialism. While travelling as far north as Scotland had not been part of her original plan, Henry couldn't resist returning to a place where she had previously received a warm welcome from friends old and new:

> Being half way to even the furthest off of our Scottish Groups, and remembering the pleasure I had had early in this year in taking part in the propaganda among those cordial bands of zealous comrades, I could not resist the temptation to intimate my readiness to visit them again if they so desired. Accordingly, on August 18th, I proceeded to Aberdeen. The bracing air of this fine northern, smokeless town refreshes the body, while the genial and truly brotherly welcome with which one is received by our Aberdonian comrades, makes a week's propaganda there both an inspiration and a privilege.[9]

This sense of love and vitality leaves a trace. As Henry wrote, she was drawn time and again to those places with which she felt an affinity. And, importantly, others felt an affinity with certain places because of previous friendly encounters like Henry's. In this way, traces of people who have organised and shared intimacies and revolutionary ideas linger and create atmospheres. The vibe of a place might be variously inviting, hostile, affecting, stirring or fearsome, and this has real implications for later activists. Legacies of friendship and the promise of a warm welcome can guide future activist routes, and in doing so create recognisable geographies of solidarity. Following Henry's tour, Aberdeen became increasingly important in Scottish anarchism: in 1895 the Aberdeen Anarchist Communist Group hosted the third conference of Scottish Anarchists. Thus Henry's impromptu visit to Aberdeen signalled the increasing importance of the area to the anarchist movement, and the friendship she found there gave her a vital boost as she continued her tour in areas where the lecturing could be more gruelling.

So the scope and direction of lecture tours like Henry's were influenced not only by topography, terrain and established transport routes but also by friendship links, radical networks and local knowledge. Henry reminds us that for the fledgling anarchist movement organisational connections, such as those that grew out of the First International, can offer only a partial view of the development of anarchist thought up to the First World War. Informal links and friendship-based networks operating across borders were fundamental to the spread of such ideas.

For instance, Ole Birk Laursen has exposed some of the junctures between Indian anti-colonialism and European anarchism, particularly ideas about insurrectionist terrorism, by looking to the personal connections made by the Indian revolutionary Virendranath Chattopadhyaya during his exilic travels in pre-First World War Europe. 'His peripatetic travels open a window onto the prefigurative politics of Indian anti-colonialism and its imaginary futures, its contact zones and shared affinities with other forms of radical internationalism, in both content and methods.'[10] Similarly, writing about the Japanese anarchist journalist Ishikawa Sanshirō (1876–1956), who lived in exile in Europe just prior to the outbreak of the First World War, Nadine Willem asks, 'what should historians make of the peregrinations of an impoverished revolutionary from East Asia in a dislocated Europe?'[11] Quite a lot, she argues. And we agree! Sanshirō and Chattopadhyaya, like many radical thinkers and doers, were shaped as much by movement, chance encounter and connection as by doctrine and training. The history of struggle is built on the ideas and actions of figures like these, moving through different places, encountering different people. Centring friendship here expands the concept of anarchism itself by showing that it was never just a form of politics concerned with the critique of state power, but rather a much more comprehensive ideological template through which to reconfigure all spheres of life: for activists on the road, the anarchism and revolutionary socialism they embodied represented a mode of participation in the world that sought to eschew hierarchical relations in all forms of life.

In the more parochial landscapes of rural Britain, attempts to embody the *life* of revolutionary socialism and to make a mass movement of it were perhaps best exemplified by the Clarion vanners. The *Clarion* newspaper was by far Britain's most popular socialist newspaper. Founded in Manchester in 1891 by Robert Blatchford and Alexander M. Thompson, the paper reached a peak circulation of 74,000 in 1907. In the same period Blachford's *Merrie England* (published in 1893) sold over two million copies. Blatchford wanted to make socialists and create fellowship. He was critical of electoral politics and his paper instead advocated direct democracy and bottom-up governance. The *Clarion* slogan, 'Fellowship is Life', borrowed from William Morris's *A Dream of John Ball*, makes clear a commitment to a relational and everyday utopianism.

In pursuit of friendship and political and social transformation, a large number of associated clubs and societies – cycling, rambling, crafts, drama and photography, as well as Cinderella Clubs and choral societies – were created in connection with the paper (of which the National Clarion Cycling Club and the Sheffield Clarion Ramblers still survive, as does the People's Theatre in Newcastle, which started in 1911 as the Newcastle Clarion Drama Club). Clarion vans, Clarion cyclists and Clarion Scouts travelled the country lecturing on socialism and selling socialist literature, and dozens of Clarion clubhouses and cafés were set up across Britain. This was very much a decentralised but collective movement, a sort of translocal solidarity movement connecting local identity with the supra-national goals of international socialism. And the approach was wildly successful. As the early twentieth-century historian George Taylor put it: 'Robert Blatchford ... can manufacture Socialists more quickly than anyone else. Tipton Limited sells more tea than any other firm, Lever sells more soap; one factory makes more boots; another more chairs. Mr Blatchford and The Clarion make more Socialists than any rival establishment.'[12]

The nebulous organisations and activities that sprung up around the Clarion were particularly invested in facilitating everyday lived socialism. Many Clarion initiatives were 'less preoccupied with political programmes than with enlarging the individual personality through creative activities, the development of "fellowship" and a group life which foreshadowed the collectivity of the socialist society for which they were striving'.[13] Most popular were the cycling clubs, which combined friendship, fun and the means via which to spread the word of socialism. Clarion cycling clubs were encouraged to compile lists of speakers able to cycle 20 to 50 miles on Saturdays and Sundays who could address public meetings in towns and villages which, as yet, had no socialist organisations.

Perhaps the next logical step from cycling socialist tours was caravan tours. The idea of a touring horse-drawn caravan for spreading political messages had been pioneered by the English Land Restoration League and the Land Nationalisation Society in the early 1890s, and in 1896 Julia Dawson suggested the Clarion adopt this mobile means in service of socialism. The first tour was a thirteen-week Clarion women's van tour starting in June of 1896. Women would travel in pairs and carry with them a tent for a local boy ('somebody's younger brother perhaps') who had 'volunteer[ed] to look after the horse, make fires and wash up dishes'.[14] The vans were equipped with a bed, a table and a fold out speaking platform, so lectures could be given just about anywhere. Van itineraries were not fixed by geography, or organised purely to cover as much ground as possible, but rather often subject to activists' feelings and friendships. Van lecturers, having the freedom of their own transport, were free to go off course to look in on friends or visit places of meaning. In this way 'the van serve[d] not only as a centre for socialist propaganda, but ... form[ed] a bond in the movement all over the country'.[15]

The Clarion movement is often thought of as a quintessentially English form of soft socialism, and one that was pretty far removed from the fiery anarchist ideas that were developing elsewhere. This is partly because of the persistence of an idea of British exceptionalism in histories of the labour movement, often attributed to the conservative aims of British trade unions, the Liberal origins of many Labour leaders, and an underlying national chauvinism about the robustness of British institutions and British commitment to constitutionalism.[16] It is also because Robert Blatchford, founder of the *Clarion* newspaper, fundamentally lost credibility as a committed internationalist following his support for the British Empire in the South African War in 1899, and for the First World War.

But using friendship as an organising principle through which to find histories of radical struggle allows us to connect these different strands. We argue that it is important to bring the Clarion movement, and the itinerant networks it produced, into conversation with the more globalised currents of the period, to reinsert the Clarion into the story of the transnational anarcho-socialist currents of the pre-First World War world. This is not as part of an effort to rehabilitate Robert Blatchford or to make grandiose claims for British socialism, but because if we think about the success of the Clarion alongside the transnational anarchist currents of the same period we start to see that it was movement, hospitality, friendship and fellowship that animated and developed the diffuse horizontalist anarchist ideas that we now recognise as important progenitors to some of the most vital radical movements of the last 40 years. The Clarion movement and the utopian and prefigurative currents that coalesced around Blatchford, Edward Carpenter, William Morris and others became unfashionable for historians of social-ism in the twentieth century – they were seen as naive, unscientific, quaint even. But there is no way to under-stand socialist ideas outside of the ways in which people lived them. It was out of this living and doing in the late nineteenth century that the socialist programmes of the twentieth century were made (even if they were often made in opposition to precisely these forms of utopianism).

The Clarion lecture tours help us to see how interna-tionalist ideas could find local and regional audiences. It was through touring lecturers from other locales that many rank-and-file socialists found their way to inter-nationalist and anti-imperialist sentiments. The Clarion vans signalled a new form of political mobility, now that lecture tours could cover more ground and stop in places that might not have a designated lecture hall or socialist space. The vans also carried socialist literature, pamphlets and posters to be passed out around the country, and the vanners collected other literature and materials from the people they met en route, which could then be redis-tributed elsewhere. In this way the hyper-mobility of travelling lecturers helped to facilitate the movement of ideas and forms of friendship that were otherwise much less accessible for a lot of people because of geography, funds or disability. Thus, like the mobile political Zine cultures explored later in this chapter, the Clarion vans embodied the political possibilities they preached; ideas were made potent by the interpersonal connections that had sustained them over long journeys, so that even when encountering these processes second- or third-hand (via a homemade pamphlet or a well-thumbed book), the invisible hand of friendship was somehow present.

## FRIENDSHIP AS THE MEANS *AND* THE MESSAGE

In many ways travelling lecturers were a functional means via which to dispatch revolutionary messages. But they were more than just a practical solution for spreading information. By the end of the nineteenth century, despite advances in other means to spread the word of socialism – increasingly affordable technologies of print and press – face-to-face lecturing remained key to generating political commitments. Travelling, hosting, hospitality, affective connections and intimate relationships *embodied* the utopian politics preached by many activists. In other words, friendship mattered: it was the means *and* the message.

Leela Gandhi has argued that 'the trope of friendship [is] the most comprehensive philosophical signifier for all those invisible affective gestures that refuse alignment along the secure axes of filiation to seek expression outside, if not against, possessive communities of belonging'.[17] Grand narratives of international revolutionary doctrines and global movements do not always allow for these affective flows, instead constraining them in networks, nodes and mappable connections for the purpose of analysis.

Sociologists have long tried to make sense of the 'invisible affective gestures' that Gandhi flags. Jennifer Mason names them affinities – potent connections in everyday life that can quite suddenly rise up and matter, sometimes fleetingly, and sometimes with enduring effect. Affinities 'are the revelation or charisma of potent connections that feel kindred in some way and in that sense they are fundamentally relational'.[18] Mason understands these affinities as 'connective charges and energies that are of interest in themselves and not because of what they connect … they constitute animate or living connections … Always something is thought to be moving, flowing, seeking, encountering, making and even forcing connection. Affinities are essentially living, and they are lived through multidimensional encounters and sensations in personal life.'[19] Like Mason we are convinced of the significance of the energies and atmospheres of connection, of interrogating *processes* by which people are drawn to each other and to collective projects. Unlike Mason, though, we are also very much interested in what these affective connections connect – in the revolutionary ideas that they can generate and spread. Here we make the case that friendship is part of a repertoire of affective gesture that has revolutionary potential precisely because it is both a connective charge *and* a political demand.

This, for us, is how people are *moved* to political conviction. This is precisely why the intimacy of the 'backstage' elements of the lecture tour could be so powerful – it was in these encounters that affinities were felt. For ordinary people in Britain, socialist and anarchist ideas could seem untethered, abstract, other worldly. But via the 'socio-atmospherics of everyday life' – an intimate moment, a flash of anger or recognition, or an affinity with an object made with care or passed along by friendly hands – a connection could be made between the big idea and the smallness of the everyday. Socialist doctrines and generic lecture platforms might not vary much from town to town, but having tea, beers, or staying over with families meant being confronted with the ineffable, surprising, sometimes thrilling, sometimes infuriating political *life* of a person or a place, and this could be a politically powerful experience, for both the host and the hosted. In this way, itinerant lecturing was a mutually constitutive form of activism.

In his *Of Hospitality* Derrida theorises the risks and impossibilities inherent in any offer or promise of hospitality. Mireille Rosello, informed by Derrida's arguments, concludes her study of postcolonial hospitality in France by suggesting that the very power of hospitality lies in its ability to challenge, to shake or to change us, and if we cannot accept this then there is no hospitality. Indeed, 'the very precondition of hospitality may require that, in some ways, both the host and the guest accept, in different ways, the uncomfortable and sometimes painful possibility of being changed by the other'.[20] In this way, mobilities are what create the intellectual foundations of revolutionary movements. Experiences of hospitality and friendship change people, producing new politics and new ideas, and that can sometimes be confronting or painful, particularly when this newness arrives unexpectedly, via a brief encounter or a friend of a friend on the road. For travelling activists and mobile revolutionaries this was part of what they hoped to produce in the friends they encountered, but it was also very often what they experienced themselves. Friendship, then, as Ole Birk Laursen writes, is where the cross-fertilisation of ideas comes into sharp focus.[21]

## PUNK AND ZINE CIRCUITS THROUGH
## THE 1990s AND 2000s

The nineteenth-century lecture tour network percolated with friendship as a form of life and politics in ways that are inseparable from the ideas that were being discussed and formulated. The more recent history of the late 1990s and early 2000s Zine and DIY Punk circuits can also illuminate such contours of radical friendship, the dense (if sometimes fleeting) bonds created, the key role of friends of friends in scaling this up, and the overt ways people within this milieu conceptualised friendship as radical. Here, we will briefly sketch out the shape of this scene from the vantage point of its manifestation in Bradford, the post-industrial British northern city where Joel grew up, to give a sense of its reach and implications. This is in no way a comprehensive overview of the Zine and DIY Punk scene of the time, but an attempt to situate what has often been dismissed as an idealistic (and cringe!) moment of musical and political organising within far longer histories of prefigurative politics, anti-capitalism and revolutionary friendship. We use these examples to build the argument of this chapter: that friendship on the move has been key to the formation of collective political subjectivities, and that political ideas take on life through interpersonal connections.

### ZINE WAVES

Zines are small self-published documents usually made with a particular spirit and aesthetic of Do It Yourself:

low-cost printing, photocopied images, anonymised authors, free or cheap publications. Zines have been historicised as emerging in different ways at key moments: in nineteenth-century pamphleteering, in 1930s Black self-publishing during the Harlem Renaissance, in the 1970s DIY Punk and 1990s Riot Grrl movements. We're interested here not simply in the Zine as an outlet for self-published, radical and marginalised writing and art, but in the physical circulation of Zines through punk touring, DIY distributors and friends of friends. Zines travel with people and become a way for them to signal their connection to certain groups, politics and scenes, but also to debate the limits and ideas of such scenes. Zines are shared, copied, responded to, sold, defaced and occasionally burnt; they are made potent by the interpersonal connections that give them meaning, and the spaces of affinity they are often gathered in. Zine fairs in the 2000s would regularly have contemporary writing mixed with photocopied essays by figures actively involved in the nineteenth-century lecture scene, people like Emma Goldman, Errico Malatesta and Lucy Parsons. In a broader sense, Zine culture has often embedded social movement history within its practices, constituting a living, fraying archive that balances the ephemerality of the physical documents with the sense of a historical thread running through.

The first official Bradford Zine Fair in 2010 featured a whole range of feminist, queer, ecological, anarchist and anti-capitalist stalls and workshops, along with a talk by Nick Toczek, whose *Wool City Rocker* Punk Zine was arguably the first to emerge from Bradford, in 1979. Many of those involved in the fair met through organising gigs and events at the 1in12 Club, one of the oldest running anarchist social centres in Europe, named after the fact that one in twelve people were fiddling the dole in Bradford at the time of its founding in 1981. 1in12 has a large anarchist library and some printing facilities, but most people made and printed Zines through municipal libraries, by sneaking printing credits at work or school, or at the local Bradford Resource Centre. There, the archive of trade union and political materials included back issues of everything from the worker's health magazine *Hazards* to the Asian Youth Movement's paper *Black Star*. Such spaces and histories influenced the localised print culture of cities like Bradford, as did the regular presence of touring musicians and political speakers, many of whom would bring publications and stories from different struggles around the world.

Zines such as *Rum Lad*, *Morgenmuffel* and *Subtext* wrote about punk touring, feminism, friendship and the politics of itinerant movement, as did the highly influential 2000s anarchist collective CrimethInc, whose books and posters could be found in a wildly large range of places.[22] Often subsequently dismissed as representing a kind of 'baby anarchism' – not focused enough on class struggle, intersectional forms of oppression or the 'real work' of political organising – such materials still provided a key entry point to radical politics for scores of young people. Similarly, the 1in12 Club would also host regular screenings of DVD *Schnews* reports: video montages of recent protests and resistance made by the Brighton-based activist news collective, who's monthly newssheet was also widely distributed.[23]

Punk bands would regularly bring small 'distros' of other people's Zines to sell at gigs, often with the message that materials could and should be photocopied for further dissemination. These covered a beguiling range of topics: ecological direct action by groups such as Earth First, radical herbalism, militant veganism, workplace organising, anti-fascist self-defence, crafts and home brewing, historic political struggles, personal diaries and poetry, queer relationality. Zines and the arguments within them could quite quickly be disseminated across a wide range of places, including towns and areas that were outside the dominant spheres of political and activist discourse. In the same way that regional music scenes took on peculiarly local forms (everyone in Bradford sounded like the hardcore ska band Capdown for about four years), certain political ideas and thinkers took on proximate significance: Joel remembers one weathered print-out of the intro to Peter Gelderloos's *How Non-Violence Protects the State* that got passed around friends in Bradford with a particular fervour, along with the huge ripples made by the *What About the Rapists?* Zine – many people's first introduction to transformative justice and accountability processes.[24] Sometimes the overlap between punk touring and Zine culture was even more overt: in 2009 the 1in12 Club hosted a leg of the 'Sister Spit: The Next Generation' tour with well-known feminist queer zinesters from the United States such as Michelle Tea and Cristy C. Road, along with locally based Em Ledge, whose *Poor Lass* and *Lola & the Cartwheels* Zines explored working-class queer feminism in the North. Similarly to the experience of nineteenth-century lecture speakers, participants in such tours

often found themselves moved and changed by the experience of encountering so many different places and people.
Tour dates and Zine distributions scaled up and travelled
through networks of friends of friends, anchored on key
venues and crash spaces, where the sense of mutuality
(however vague) and activity within the 'scene' allowed for
travel to and from places where 'arts funding' and dispos-
able incomes were scarce.

## GIVING UP ACTIVISM

Around the early to mid 2000s, a number of punk-focused
Zines turned towards political analysis in more overt ways.
The influential punk rock Zine *Last Hours* (fka *Rancid
News*) changed its tagline in 2009 from 'Radical culture
and punk rock' to 'Creative resistance', with special issues
on the G20 protests and police violence. This followed on
from people involved with the Zine helping to establish
the London Zine Symposium, an annual hub for the
scene from 2005–11 (alongside the long-running London
Anarchist Book Fair). Such spaces were key for gathering,
reflection and debate on the central political struggles of
the time – particularly the anti-globalisation movement,
the Iraq War protests and the emerging No Borders
movement. Summits such as the G20, G7 and G8 – the
latter of which was held in Edinburgh in 2005 and acted as
a catalyst for various activist groups in Scotland – brought
a swirling mix of people, ideas and physical materials into
motion. Again, diffuse interpersonal connections were
key, operating across squats, social centres and online
message boards. These were anonymised in the sense

that you just had to be a 'friend of a friend' or be adjacent to such spaces to be offered up a couch, a cigarette or a contact number for the next trip. It's worth remembering that YouTube arrived only that year, in 2005, Instagram in 2010, and features such as Facebook Live (and more widespread 4G streaming capacity) only in 2015 – so the sharing of footage and reportage from such events required far more direct, analogue dissemination. Whilst the connections and movements forged through anti-globalisation protests were vast, the particular focus on mobility and physical direct action also began to be critiqued during this period.

The key, anonymous, text at the heart of this push-back was called 'Give Up Activism', appearing in 1999 for the first time in the *Do or Die* Zine and then shared as its own Zine with a postscript for a long time after. The piece situates the 'activist' as patronising in their assumption of 'expertise', cliquey, isolated and lacking analyses of class and work – 'activists' failed to embed themselves in communities and workplaces where they would engage in change in their day-to-day lives, instead zipping around international sites of contestation and parachuting in for brief forays.[25] The discussion this provoked had a big impact on lots of people we both knew at the time, linked to an upsurge in interest in groups like the Zapatistas and ideas of autonomy that felt particularly tied to locality and space. Joel remembers – after he moved to Glasgow and got involved in the No Borders orientated Unity Centre – one friend telling him that they had decided to move back to the city after 'activist travelling' and intended to stay 'for at least ten years', because 'that's how we need to conceive of building long-term power and community in a particular place'. This critique got mixed with various others around disability justice, differential possibilities of mobility within the stratified and racist layers of immigration control, and white saviourism.

Debates around 'activist tourism' were also rife in key sites of struggle such as the Calais migrant camp, ZAD anti-airport occupations and the Athens squat scene, though connections to these places (at least in Glasgow) were maintained in a way that didn't happen with other anti-globalisation era sites. The circulation of people through No Borders networks, including those directly involved in the struggle for immigration papers, also drew on punk and squat scenes, and networks of friends across these sites would often be the first to communicate bits of news or put people in touch with a someone who'd made it across the border but needed support. Zines from Calais and other border regime sites circulated too, often in multiple languages, and reading groups and trainings at places like Unity Centre would draw on these, along with new interventions such as the 2014 *Accomplices Not Allies* Zine, 'an Indigenous perspective' on 'abolishing the ally industrial complex'.[26] The move to online webzines, blogs and social media posting coincided, then, with challenges to 'activist tourism' – signalling a shift to a more sedentary era of political work.

While the critiques levelled against the anti-globalisation and 'summit hopping' era are important, it seems that something can also be lost in a wholesale abandoning of motion and physical interconnection between different geographic sites of struggle. As both the nineteenth-century lecture tours and 2000s Zine and Punk circuits show, building possibilities for material, mutual sharing of space and ideas is key to fertile political movements. In the early days of the Unity Centre, news would filter in from friends in Calais almost every day, and people would come and go from places in ways that allowed for a steady trickle of information and interconnection. This seemed to slow down dramatically around 2014–15, no doubt linked to political shifts in relation to the migrant camps and the lead up to the Brexit vote, but also to a deliberate 'localism' that could end up making people feel siloed in their locale. Imagining possible ways of generating interconnectedness across mobile sites of struggle within the confines of the deeply differentiated, racist and ableist ways in which people are prevented from moving requires real effort and risk. But we can attend to specificity and embrace vital attachments to place without abandoning interconnection. We shouldn't underestimate the vitality of new experiences, of new people, places and atmospheres, when developing political strategies.

Throughout the recent history of Zines and the punk and activist movements sketched here, people have also proactively debated the question of political friendship and interconnection. The aforementioned *Accomplices Not Allies* Zine fits into a longer history of active debates around the terminology needed to describe and prefigure our political relatedness. Zines such as Sandra Jeppesen's *Queering Heterosexuality* connected discussions of friendship, polyamory and political struggle to personal reflections on sexuality.[27] Lee P's 2013 Zine *PALS: The Radical Possibilities of Friendship* quotes Jeppesen and the writer Dean Spade in articulating an ethos at the heart of these texts: 'treat your friends like lovers and your lovers like friends'.[28] There is a sad irony – considering how focused on sex and romance much non-monogamy discourse has since become – in how focused these influential texts were on dismantling the assumed primacy of romantic ties, expanding notions of desire and sex, and building more attentiveness and commitment into friendship. More recently, Zines have been central to the political formulations of trans writers, with the ground-breaking *Radical Transfeminism* (edited by Nat Raha) and Mira Bellwether's *Fucking Trans Women* Zines, discussing trans sexuality, sociality and political activity.[29] Through all these examples we see a shifting articulation of what it means to build political community, as well as the means of expressing this, through the circulation of ideas (often radically self-actualising ones about healthcare and sex), physical material and people. Friendship and queerness as forms of life that both challenged normative ideas of family and prefigured other ways of collective being were expressed here in multiple ways: words on a page, a sofa to sleep on, a lift to somewhere you needed to be.

\* \* \*

In drawing a connection between travelling activists in provincial Britain in the 1880s and Zine-making punks in the Bradford of the 2000s, we've casually traversed a vast and varied political landscape (not to mention the entirety of the twentieth century). We don't mean to suggest that these vastly different modes of organising hinged on friendship in precisely the same way, but rather that friendship and mobility often intersect quite powerfully in the development of revolutionary politics, and that this can take various forms. The mobility and forms of hospitality that we argue have been so key in developing and enacting revolutionary ideas were not just about closed networks of individual friends, or cliquish access to personal and privileged networks (though of course we can find evidence of these dynamics across revolutionary movements forever), but rather about how the processes via which ideas were spread, documented and given voice or meaning were imbued with friendship and care, even if the individuals involved weren't friends themselves. Individual friendships were important, but friendship as a way of life had a much wider reach.

# CHAPTER FOUR

# Old Friends

Steve McQueen's *Small Axe* (2020) series tells stories of London's West Indian communities in postwar Britain. The anthology takes us through the lives and neighbourhoods of Black mothers agitating for educational reform via the Caribbean Education and Community Workers Association in the 1970s; Black British activists frequenting Notting Hill's Mangrove Restaurant in the late 1960s; young lovers at a reggae house party in West London in the early 1980s; and others besides. Laura watched the series in January of 2021, during the third national Covid-19 lockdown in England. Having just moved to a new city, grieving a recent loss, and coming to terms with a changed world, those few months are tinged with melancholy and loneliness. In such a context, *Small Axe* felt particularly warm. Not fluffy, or easy, or saccharine – but warm with the richness of lives lived in collectivity and connection, despite hardship. Thick with various forms of intergenerational associational cultures, McQueen's stories foreground dense and complex bonds, often in difficult circumstances. These tales are rarely linear, often time-hopping, and spliced with real footage from the past.

Episode 5, 'Alex Wheatle', opens in Wormwood Scrubs prison, London, in 1981. Alex Wheatle, or Yardman Irie as he is known when on the mic, has been incarcerated following his role in the 1981 Brixton Uprising. An early prison scene sees a frustrated Alex breakdown in his cell-mate's arms. Simeon, a Rastafarian at least two decades Alex's senior, forces Alex's searching fists and raging limbs into a fierce embrace – 'listen man, i want to hear, what's your story?' he demands soothingly, to which Alex replies, 'i ain't got no fricking story'.

And indeed, we never get the whole story. Through flash-backs, though, we learn that Alex grew up without a family. Bounced around between foster homes and made to feel shame and confusion about his identity, Alex often appears disconnected from those around him. Through an older kid, Dennis, Alex learns how to navigate South London as a teenager; he learns how to walk and talk – 'to be more Brixton [and] to strut as a Black man strut', as Dennis puts it. But it is not until he meets Simeon that Alex embraces his own story. Simeon's questions allow us to visit moments from Alex's past – traumas inflicted by cruel carers, a vora-cious appetite for music, and a swift politicisation following the events of the New Cross Massacre. Through Simeon, Alex is opened up to deep intergenerational connections and discovers the radical riches of history.

Simeon is explicit in his desire to connect Alex's past with his own, and to connect them both to much longer historical lineages, all while remaining oriented towards the future. 'My thoughts long been trained pon the youth, man', says Simeon, as he offers up his personal library (the cell is lined with books) as well as his friendship, 'I have to play my part cos me know the future is yours.'

Alex: 'some future, dread'.

Simeon: 'hear me now, Alex, you see if you don't know your past then you won't know your future ... me can recommend you start by reading this here one here so, the Black Jacobins, by Cyril Lionel Robert James, jah know he will show you the way!'

'Alex Wheatle' is a moving piece of cinema because it communicates the value of cross-generational generosity. Intergenerational connections quietly vibrate through-out the series, but here in just a few short lines McQueen explicitly connects radical histories and lineages with friendship. As the real-life Alex Wheatle acknowledged after the films were released, 'whatever I achieve in this old writing game is down to the conversion I experienced under Simeon in Wormwood Scrubs ... I will be forever grateful to him.'[1]

McQueen's film recalls forms of guiding friendship that many of us have experienced in the company of an elder. And yet, despite how formative these friendships can be, they are often also fraught, particularly when it comes to politics. Watching *Small Axe* we are left wondering why, if cross-generational friendships are so vital, they can often be so hard. Why is it so easy to mis-connect and misun-derstand across generational divides?

\* \* \*

Stuart Hall, reflecting in 2010 on the obstacle of gener-ation in the founding of the New Left in the late 1950s, suggested that:

> the New Left represented the coming together of two related but different traditions – also of two politi-cal experiences or generations. One was the tradition

I would call, for want of a better term, communist humanism ... The second is perhaps best described as an independent socialist tradition, whose centre of gravity lay in the left student generation of the 1950s and which maintained some distance from 'party' affiliations ... This was a difference not of age but of formation – a question of *political generations*, within which the [Second World] War constituted the symbolic dividing line.[2]

Hannah Proctor refers to Hall's characterisation when recounting her own political coming of age and the historical specificity of the generation in which she came to political consciousness, very much shaped by Britain's invasion of Iraq in 2003 and the global financial crash of 2008.[3] Throughout history, activists and revolutionaries have situated themselves in this way. There is nothing new in feeling politically shaped by one's generation, and, as a result, feeling very aware of dividing lines – wars, epidemics, regime changes – that are not always easily bridged.

Right now, the startling and increasing age segregation in cities across the world (a report in 2020 found that Britain is one of the world's most age-segregated countries[4]) – coupled with a British media that has spent the last 15 years doggedly pitting retirees against students; millennials and gen Z-ers against boomers; and older cis women against younger trans people – is contributing to a sense of relentless generational antagonism that plays out with often dangerous consequences (particularly for trans people). Right now, much of the political and the media class feels generationally distant from a Tik-Toker generation that is creating and consuming ideas in very different ways. These generational divides can open up what often feel like irreparable rifts in left movements. We are not, of course, suggesting that we could or should do away with generational solidarities or shared generational experiences (although sometimes, as Penelope Lively put it, 'chronology irritates me'[5]), but rather that we can also find important examples and histories of the relational and reparative function of *cross-generational* solidarities. Here we want to explore how friendship can be a politically powerful way of talking and learning across time, connecting past, present and future struggles.

## ENCOUNTERS ACROSS TIME

Encounters across time have always been of particular value to marginalised people. For queer people, 'long encouraged by mainstream norms to understand themselves as people with no collective, nourishing past and no realistic or hopeful future', these encounters work in two ways.[6] They can come through lived intergenerational friendships between queer elders and younger queers – a powerful motif in the real and fictionalised lives of queer people everywhere, made potent partly because of the wonder of the existence of queer elders at all, of people *who survived*. Then there is the more expansive and imagined intergenerational friendship that comes through finding queer histories that reach out across time with powerful affect. The relative scarcity of the queer archive – a product of lives being made secret and cut short, and of histories forcibly erased and excluded – can make the sense of affinity experienced when encountering queer pasts feel revolutionary. Finding past people with whom we feel affinity is a way of disrupting histories and narratives that insist on the marginalisation of certain stories: finding a friend in the past is all the more powerful when you have been told that you have no precedent, that your existence is unnatural or unwelcome.

In this way, then, friendship is a fundamental part of the revolutionary imagination – pursuing friendship is always about continued education, always relational, always in motion, always striving (you can't just do the comrade exam and then be qualified for life). Lynne Segal argues that we need friendship across the lifecycle and across generations,

> if only because old age sooner or later increases the likelihood of new forms of dependence ... forms of dependency are a part of the human condition, and we only gain any sense of ourselves through our ties to others. Yet it is just those ties of dependence that we tend to repudiate entering adulthood in cultures such as ours, where what we are taught to value is the notion of autonomy and self-sufficiency above all else.[7]

Practising intergenerational friendship, then, is both a practical way to counter such notions and a necessary means through which to encourage precisely the forms of interdependence necessary for building alternative movements. Organiser Mariame Kaba put it well when she said:

Political education is so, so important. Very important. Not in a way that you can just put it to the side, as
something we add on. It is at the core of how we're going
to grow our movement … I also think that if you're a
veteran organiser it is your duty, I believe, to come into
spaces with an open heart and an open ear and not to
go in there with your arms crossed, ready to pounce,
on how these young folks are doing everything wrong
all the time. That is not productive, it isn't helpful … I
realise that part of what happened over the years is that
for some veteran organisers they do feel slighted … the
age group of folks who are 45 and older is absolutely
decimated in terms of who remains in organising …
The reason that happened is there were real forces that
depleted our ranks. Those forces were Reagan. Those
forces were Clinton. Those forces were the HIV/AIDS
epidemic … There's a lack of people right now in that
age group with lot of experience around organising for
younger people, for millennials and others, to turn to.
I think people get upset when they're not called upon,
sometimes, if they're veteran organisers to offer their
suggestions and everything, but I always tell people that
the most important thing is just to build relationships
with young folks.[8]

This learning and doing must necessarily happen between
people of different ages and formations – it comes through
knowing each other, older and younger, and through
knowing history. At times, cliques of age and formation can foreclose intergenerational connections. Hard
dividing lines can make the past feel old, inadequate and

irrelevant, and the future feel impenetrable, untethered and terrifying.

Here is where the archive is so important. The archive (and we use the term expansively, both formal and informal) is a fundamental part of political education: a living link between old and new. Artist and RUKUS! archive curator Ajamu X emphasises the affective, the sonic and the bodily in the archive – 'our nipples and dicks and arses are also archives'.[9] He asks how we might converse with these *active* archives, because, in his words, 'when I touch the archive, the archive also touches me'.[10] Stuart Hall stressed the 'living archive', whose construction 'must be seen as an on-going, never-completed project'.[11] For Ann Cvetkovich forms of queer intimacy are an 'emotional experience and the[ir] memory demand[s] and produce[s] an unusual archive, one that frequently resists the coherence of narrative or that is fragmented'.[12] Finding ways to transmit these intimate histories is key to radical struggle; formalised political parties and institutions readily pass on their histories and have the infrastructure with which to do so, but 'non-aligned activists and thinkers have only our snatched and fleeting reconstructions of seizing the moments when change seems possible'. Therefore, 'the transmission of generational histories can foster ways of communicating as times change. Older radicals and younger rebels have equal need of such history'.[13]

We want to suggest that friendships themselves are archives of all the informal, intimate and irreplicable affects and ideas that create revolutionary subjectivities. Studying past friendship and feeling friendship in the archive allows us – in small ways – to access these scram-

bled and valuable records, to gently pull on the thread
of history and in doing so generate a ripple that causes a
distant bell to ring in another time or place.

## BEFRIENDING THE DEAD

In *The Friend*, published posthumously in 2003, Alan
Bray finds friendship in an archive of sorts. In the 1980s,
in the chapel of Christ's College, Cambridge, he discov-
ered a tomb shared by two men, John Finch (1626–82)
and Thomas Baines (c.1624–81). The tomb featured
stirring imagery dedicated to their friendship, with portraits of the two friends linked by a knotted cloth. These
seventeenth-century friends reached out to Bray, and
researching their lives revealed a long lineage of friendships, intimacies and desires that offered powerful
examples for those involved in the gay liberation movements of the late twentieth century. For Bray, piecing
together the lives of friends long gone became a personal
act of remembrance and mourning for his own friends
who were dying of AIDS: 'I think I was seeking among the
tombs of the dead those lost friends; I would not let them
go: and with the guiding hand of scholarship and the eye
of a historian, against all expectations I found such friendship there in those monuments.'[14]

The Lesbian Herstory Archives provides stirring tombs
of different kinds, no less ready to awaken the political
imagination and to prompt feelings of grief, defiance and
friendship. Founded in Brooklyn, New York in 1974, the
key principles of the archive are:

- Archival skills are taught one generation of Lesbians to another, breaking the elitism of traditional archives;
- The Archives is committed to the political struggles of all Lesbians and their communities;
- The Archives is dedicated to building intergenerational bridges among Lesbian communities to deepen the understanding of what Lesbian experiences mean in different contexts and in different historical periods.[15]

These principles are explicitly concerned with creating feelings of friendship, community and care for those shaping, contributing to and accessing the archive across generations. When Laura visited in the spring of 2024 the archive felt immediately distinctive – like a place where histories went to live rather than to die. The archive explicitly prompts visitors to roll up their sleeves and rifle freely through the collections. There are no allocated seats, no gloves, no maximum number of items to be viewed, no rules against drinking water or talking or spreading things out on the floor. Anyone can book a three-hour unsupervised slot. Upon arrival there is a short tour given (usually) by an older lesbian who knows the archive in the enviable way that only comes through the labours of time and love. There were people visiting the archive and snapping photos for their own scrapbooks, others crafting Zines. It's hard not to romanticise a space such as the LHA – there is something so immediately tactile, DIY, defiant and scrappy about the collection. Sometimes political feeling really is about the form as well as the content – the affective experience of rifling through a filing cabinet of explicit photos, or sitting on the floor leafing through the diarised scrawlings of Audre Lorde, or piecing together a conversation drawn out across the letters pages of a dozen issues of *On Our Backs* by laying them out across all the surfaces in the room, creates a different form of intellectual engagement, one that is very much animated by feelings of togetherness, of a shared project.

For the Jamaican anthropologist and curator David Scott, the form of the letter, and the practice of writing letters to friends no longer around – letters that could never be sent – was part of the power of friendship in developing his intellectual outlook. Scott was a friend and interlocutor of Stuart Hall. Both scholars of cultures, ideas and political theory, and both born and raised in Jamaica, the two were of different generations, different political formations (Hall b. 1932, Scott b. 1958). Scott's imaginative exercise in friendship allowed him to talk and think across time, across generations, to think through his own contemporary moment, with the help of an old friend. The book that resulted was 'an epistolary way of continuing an intellectual relationship with Stuart Hall in the wake of his passing.'[16] It celebrates Hall's uniquely powerful voice and intellectual orientation – concerned as much with giving as receiving, as much with listening as speaking. Scott insists that friendship 'does not presume a convergence of views, agreement, but rather reciprocally shelters differences. What intellectual friendship aims at is the hermeneutic attitude of clarification.'[17] This process of clarification appears throughout the book as Scott highlights the intellectual tensions between himself and Hall

– their varied intellectual allegiances to the writers and theorists of the past. In displaying and examining these tensions, Scott suggests that, if harnessed through an ethos of listening (which he argues is precisely what friendship can allow), such tension is able to give way to a powerful kind of dialogical thinking:

> Stuart, I want to suggest that the letter is potentially the literary embodiment of a quality of relationship that might be called, simply, friendship. As a way of keeping company with special others, the letter seems to me uniquely able to disclose, or, less passively, to enact, some of the relational sentiments and virtues we commonly think of as internal to friendship ... You'll begin to see what I mean, Stuart, if you think, for example, of the published correspondence between ... Hannah Arendt and two very different long-lasting friends of hers from two very different literary-philosophic and geopolitical worlds: Mary McCarthy, on the one hand, and Karl Jaspers, on the other ... You didn't much read Arendt, I know, Stuart (didn't quite see the point, you once told me). But I will hope to persuade you along the way ... that ... Arendt was a great, and more, an instructive, believer in the powers and promise of friendship, of what friendship potentially secures and enables in a relatively protected space that is neither exactly home nor world, neither exactly private nor public, but an unsystematic overlapping of both together.[18]

Scott conjures the generosity that comes with friendship – giving someone the benefit of the doubt as they work through ideas, and expecting the same in return. The antithesis of the instant Twitter hot take/take down. The idea of clarification, of protected space, and Scott's persistent use of rhetorical questions through the book – directed to Hall but also to us – are reminiscent of Sarah Schulman's characterisation of a friend as someone who asks probing questions, someone who enables exploration, who challenges received ideas but welcomes difference:

> The phrase 'chosen family' makes me quake with fear. I prefer the far more valuable term, 'friend'. A true friend can be a blood or legal relation. They can be in the same clique or neighborhood or workplace. They can belong to the same racial, cultural, religious, or national group. But a true 'friend' asks the right questions about the category itself, and thereby transcends it. A true friend has the conversation.[19]

Here Schulman also makes a powerful point about friendship being a category of deep and valuable commitment, one that we shouldn't need to elevate to 'family' in order that it be understood as such. As Scott's correspondence with Hall makes clear, the kinds of conversations that Schulman alludes to can outlast a lifetime. The practice of writing letters to dead friends is not new, though, and Scott's assertion that this form of friendship aims at a 'hermeneutic attitude of clarification' feels very appropriate for a pair of friends – Sarah Savage and Jane Ward Hunt – living in the Welsh-English borderlands in the early eighteenth century. Amanda Herbert has painstakingly reconstructed Savage and Hunt's friendship through

rare and rich archives scattered across multiple institutions on both sides of the Atlantic. Through the two
women's diaries and letters, most of which were written
from Savage to Hunt in the four decades *after* Hunt's death
in 1716, Herbert was able to reconstruct a dialogue that,
like Scott's, was imagined but no less reciprocal because of
it. Hunt's passing was so painful to Savage that, 'in order
to retain some sense of her presence, she began writing
to her deceased friend, quoting Hunt from memory and
then responding to the dead woman's ideas as if the two
confidants – one living, and one dead – were having a
conversation.'[20]

For 36 years, until her own death in 1752, Savage con-
versed with Hunt in this way. She referred to this practice
quite consciously, explaining that it was through 'Mrs.
H's Papers in which she being dead yet speaketh.'[21] When
Savage faced moral dilemmas or needed a good example
on which to model her own behaviour, she looked to Jane
Hunt. Savage also spoke to Hunt and conjured her voice
when she worried about her associations with neighbours
and friends. Savage's Dissenting faith and her inability to
conform to traditional Anglican practices of religion and
sociability meant that her relationships with many people
in her community were often marked by misunderstand-
ing and mistrust. 'When Savage expressed concern about
getting along with her neighbours in her diaries, she
spoke with Hunt in order to decide upon a good course of
action.'[22] For Savage, then, friendship was a mode of intellectual and affective exploration, an orientation towards
deliberation and rumination which, when practised,
could generate care and community.

Perhaps the time-travelling and cross-generational dimensions of these friendships remind us that there *is* time to ask questions, that we don't need to have all the answers now, and that we can always speak to and think with friends who are not of the same age or formation. Indeed, that it might even be possible to think through these things *collectively*, relationally, even with people no longer around. What these letters, and all the letters in the lesbian archive give us, is a sense of the passage of time, the accumulation of friendships, and the wealth of care and knowledge they can communicate to us. In all these instances, friendship and its associated affects provided a way of talking to the past, with a view to formulating political ideas and identities in the present.

## FLEETING FRIENDSHIP AND ANONYMOUS ATTACHMENTS

While some of the forms of connection we have explored so far can last beyond a lifetime, when thinking through the intergenerational influences that have been important in our own political lives, we are struck by the significance of often fleeting moments of intergenerational connection animated in pubs, clubs, cafés and music venues. These fleeting friendships constitute an 'ever-shifting and intricate mosaic of small-scale social relations and subcultures',[23] and in our increasingly age-segregated cities such spaces and moments represent important links through time. These connections are part of the intellectual and affective infrastructure of our political lives, and they challenge the pervasive idea that the young and the old are doomed to political antagonism.

Scott Haine calls these ambiguous friendships 'unseen solidarities'.[24] Writing about the phenomena of the 'café-friend' in nineteenth-century Paris, Haine describes how, through neighbourhood spaces, 'a new type of friendship [emerged] that was simultaneously intimate and anonymous'.[25] These often politicised friendships could be sustained for many months or even longer, without the 'friends' ever exchanging full names or contact details. This kind of encounter is often intergenerational: the woman you bump into every Thursday at the pub and discuss the latest Labour fuck-up with; the fella that runs the bookshop down the road who recommends titles that lead you in new directions; the ritual of the heated debate that takes place with the same handful of people who frequent the same café for a Saturday fry-up. There is something freeing in talking about both feelings and political dreams or madcap ideas with people who are not otherwise linked to your everyday life. Feelings of affinity can produce quite striking forms of generosity, which, as with other forms of friendship, can allow for discussion and divergence in ways that would be much more difficult to achieve in an official meeting or an online platform. In café-friendship there is often a shared warmth that 'shelters difference'.

New languages of solidarity arise through these friendships. For neighbourhood drinkers in nineteenth-century Paris, as today, 'relations often became codified by the use of nicknames. Probably over a toast, café habitues might receive nicknames from the proprietor or other patrons.'[26] These names displaced the person's real name so completely that when the police asked clients about fellow frequenters they could only identify them by their nick-names. For example:

> Mathias Hermann, a labourer, knew Ferdinand Chris-tian, also a labourer, only by his nickname of 'the paw'. Marie Ardisson, a registered prostitute (*fille soumise*), referred to two habitué of a café on the rue des Maturins solely by their café nicknames: 'There was in the wine merchant's an individual who carried the nickname of "the carp" (*la volige*), lover of a person called "the pock-marked one" (*la grelée*) who sold potatoes' … Many of the designations such as '*turio*', '*aglaré*', '*charlot*' and '*pin-sonneau*' have no fully comprehensible meaning outside the specific café context in which they were coined.[27]

This language of friendship creates new forms of sociabil-ity that are not defined by the usual social markers of status or wealth or family ties. Instead, they are built organically around a different logic: a logic of friendship. Haine also describes how patrons might bring food or spare clothing for one another, offer to help one another move house or fix their bicycle or their shoes, or be a witness at a café-friend's marriage or baptism. In this way, sociability and mutual aid were intertwined in café friendships. The development of the working-class café as a forum within which new friendships could develop facilitated cul-tural exchange and transmission between different social groups and across different ages and occupations. 'These friendships did not produce a narrow subculture closed within the confines of craft or occupation but, rather, a supple sociability that adapted to changes within the structure of the working class.'[28] Café friendships reflected and accommodated changes in the urban environment (like those wrought by Hausmannisation, for example) by providing strangers with a shared set of rituals for inter-action. This was a protected social space that was 'neither exactly home nor world'. Instead, a third space.

The café therefore played an important role in politi-cal life. It is no coincidence that the organisation of the Paris Commune of 1871 was 'rooted in neighbourhoods' and relied on the politics of association, both formal and informal. The kaleidoscopic world of neighbourhood café-friendships created and sustained the necessary sol-idarity networks and cultures within which 'opponents of the Empire socialized and learned to trust or detest one another'.[29] In Britain, interested observers noted that the kinds of unseen solidarities forged through café-friend-ships could help explain the Parisian working classes' particular 'periodic capacity for mass mobilization and revolution'. In June 1871, after the fall of the Commune, the London working-class newspaper, *The Bee Hive*, asked 'what had allowed the workers to rise as one during the Commune?' The author marvelled at their Parisian coun-terparts who had been able to build such a movement *without* the freedom to organise a political society, openly hold large meetings or march in a procession or protest. *The Bee Hive* journalist went on to conclude that the explanation must lie in the fact that 'the ground was pre-pared by talk at workshops and cabarets'.[30]

As a result of these informal political cultures, these spaces were often subject to undercover or covert policing (as they are today, as we will see in the next chapter). While this could detract from the vitality of such spaces, the intimate anonymity that characterised these friendships could also serve as a useful means of plausible deniability: 'political discussion and organization could be conducted under cover of the mundane activities of eating, drinking and talking. The ephemeral nature of café sociability supplied participants with an excellent reason for denying the seriousness of their words and actions.'[31] In other words, here friendship was made powerful because of the ease with which people are often inclined to relegate it in the hierarchy of human relationships. More fool them.

## THE ANTI-FAMILY TREE

As we discussed in Chapter 1, the Kurdish concept of *hevaltî* offers an important example of how a revolutionary society can be built around friendship. *Hevaltî*, and the practice of friendship that is so central to everyday life in Rojava, also has important intergenerational functions. Women guerrillas in the Kurdish Women's Freedom Movement (which includes the Free Women's Units and the Women's Protection Units, both affiliated to the PKK) commit to celibacy, and 'instead of heterosexual eroticism, a diffuse and intense eroticism is lived in the mountains as people passionately orient themselves toward nature, friendship, politics, and combat, all of which enable them to strongly sense the animating force of life'.[32]

*Hevaltî* is practised, taught and passed down through generations of revolutionaries. Social reproduction in this revolutionary society does not pass through bloodlines, families or succession. Instead, history and memory are passed on through generations via friendship and education. Here is the anti-family tree in action. Women guerrillas shed their names and are reborn when they commit to the mountains. In doing so they reject familial forms of reproduction and create new forms of generational and intergenerational coexistences, attachments and intimacies:

> With their newly acquired names and their status as friends, the guerrillas who were born and raised in a strictly filial society find themselves in a state (not unlike queer communities) where they need to 'invent from A to Z' the ethics by which they will relate to each other and to others. As revolutionaries, they need to enact transformative intimacies with people of the same sex or different sexes, different age groups, and different collectivities.[33]

Having made this separation from the family – 'a necessary condition for women to attain freedom' – guerrillas become part of a new history of struggle and in doing so create a new generation. In diverting the power of the nuclear family, and instead centring friendship, they 'interrupt women's suffering in the household transmitted from generation to generation and enable the making of a new women's history and memory'.[34]

This commitment to revolutionary friendship is a way to undercut the primacy of the family and of patriarchal notions of family honour. Rojava is a women's revolution, and its guiding principles are anti-patriarchal and anti-hierarchical. At the heart of the revolution is the idea (articulated by Abdullah Öcalan) that in order to create a just society you must completely transform social relations. Under the auspices of the umbrella women's organisation Kongreya Star (Star Congress), the women's movement reaches into every aspect of life. An important part of this is the Mala Jinê (women's houses). These are places where women of all ages can come to work through problems in the community. Largely led by older women – women who came of age and lived under Assad's dictatorial regime – the Mala Jinê are central to the community; instead of the police or the court system, they are often the first port of call when disputes arise.[35]

Through the Mala Jinê there is a clear sense of the relationship between intergenerationality, political education and *hevaltî*. Here we see women attending to and educating one another across a considerable generational shift which cuts across the establishment of Rojava in 2013 and the profound transformations that resulted. As Bookchin, Şahin and Sitrin observed, 'there was this sense of cross-generational unity between [these women]'.[36] The elders are proud of the role they played in raising children who could now live in a liberated society, and proud to pass on stories of how the revolution began and of the oppression it overcame. Likewise, the young people are proud to be able to teach their elders about the ways in which the revolution is continually unfolding around them. Having lived through different regimes, the elders are determined and dexterous, and carry valuable histories; the youngers, having only really known Rojava, bring confidence, commitment and energy. The practice of *hevaltî* across this generational divide, then, undermines common assumptions about the radicalism of youth and the conservatism of old age, and instead manifests as a powerful social, martial and political force.

The revolutionary commitment of the Kurdish Women's Freedom Movement to friendship as a way of life in some ways feels worlds away from the imagined abstract *feeling* of friendship experienced in the archive when encountering histories which prompt powerful feelings of affinity. A marked feature of *hevaltî* is its ethics of *impersonality*. This is pursued deliberately in order to discourage identitarian politics. According to the PKK, personal friendship (that is, friendship not as a position or a guiding commitment but as an individual relationship with a significant other or others) can very easily become exclusionary on the ground of identity. 'One way in which impersonality in friendship is achieved is through assignments, which keep "friends" in the movement constantly on the move and render them literally homeless.' Much like the tireless socialist lecturers from Chapter 2, 'in the Kurdish Movement any *heval* [friend] can be assigned to anywhere which makes it hard to continue personalized friendships formed in one assignment. On the contrary, she is expected to be a general friend to all, to care for them and be committed to a mutual transformation wherever she goes.'[37]

In contrast to this ideal pursued by the guerrilla women of Rojava, it is often identity, or a feeling of identification, that produces affinities with friends of the past and with histories of struggle. And yet we can usefully draw a link between these two quite different forms of friendship. For the dykes seeking a past in the Lesbian Herstory Archives, and for the guerrillas fighting for the future of Rojava, the search for friendship and a commitment to its practice interrupts formidable currents of power and patriarchy that pass from generation to generation, and diverts this power to new ends. This commitment to friendship offers alternative lineages and draws on alternative forms of social reproduction. These are all forms of friendship that invite questions, seek truth and embrace motion and difference. They open us up to mutual transformation, to the possibility of being reconfigured, and they involve 'both equality and differentiation ... harmony as well as conflict, recognition as well as criticism'.[38]

In a moving piece about a visit to Rojava, Harry Waveney connects *hevaltî* to the themes celebrated in Auld Lang Syne.[39] For Waveney, a founding member of Kurdish Solidarity Cymru, the revolution in Rojava 'is more than the region's confederated democratic communes, its academies, its "women's houses", or its workers' co-ops. The Rojava revolution is *hevaltî* generalised, and it is not limited to the borders of Northeast Syria. It exists within those who fight for it, worldwide. It is friendship rendered at the level of politics.'[40] Waveney arrived in Rojava from rural Wales, and through his experience of *hevaltî*, and endless cups of tea (or *çay*) drunk with *hevals* undertaking brutal hunger strikes, he was reminded of the traditional Scottish poem. Auld Lang Syne is a call to remember long-standing friendships that have passed. Through it we are invited to share a drink with friends, to recall old friends, and in doing so to connect to each other, to generations of friends long gone and to those that will come after:

And there's a hand my trusty friend!
And give me a hand o' thine!
And we'll take a right good-will draught,
for auld lang syne

Auld Lang Syne seems a fitting place to close the chapter. Differences in generation and formation, the passage of time and the feelings provoked by difficult histories, can all make friendship feel fraught at times. And yet it is often through precisely these themes that friendship can also feel at its warmest and most tender. As Lynne Segal writes: 'for certain, our political hopes may continue to be disappointed or defeated much of the time. Yet here again, in collective endeavours as in personal life, the conscious effort to understand and communicate the near inevitability of a certain tragic residue in the wake of political struggles helps keep us alive to life itself.'[41] What the different intergenerational friendship forms explored in this chapter share is precisely this commitment to communicating across time, to thinking beyond the temporalities in which we find ourselves, and to connecting with old wisdom as we collectively construct new ways of being together.

# Conversation with Luke de Noronha

*Laura met Luke de Noronha in year seven (2001) at Priest-nall School in Stockport. Over the years their friendship has come in and out of view – and it was friendship as the subject of intellectual inquiry that brought them back into contact, when Luke submitted a piece for a 'Radical Friend-ship' series that Laura created for History Workshop Online. Luke was also the friend in common who connected Laura and Joel back in 2021!*

*In his work Luke has written about 'bad friends', or at least the ways in which friendship is rendered 'bad' or 'worthless' by the border regime. He is the author of* Deporting Black Britons: Portraits of Deportation to Jamaica *(2020) and co-author of* Against Borders: The Case for Abolition *(2022) and* Empire's Endgame: Racism and the British State *(2021).*

*This is an edited version of a conversation that took place in November 2024.*

**Laura**: Hello old friend! It's so interesting that through our long arc of friendship, somehow at this point we've ended up overlapping again, despite very different trajectories and disciplinary backgrounds. I'm not sure what it means but there is something heartwarming about it!

**Luke**: Yeah I agree, it's a long history! Our parents were friends, or at least they were in each other's orbits to a certain extent: living in the same neighbourhood, sending their kids to the same school. And all lefties, or at least left-orientated.

**Laura**: They were sort of at the edges of a similar world. Now I understand these shared histories as the kinds of webs of intergenerational connections that have really influenced my politics, and that we grew up with even if we weren't immediately conscious of it.

**Luke**: Yeah and I think those longer friendships often help to prompt new connections in unexpected ways. That's where *Empire's Endgame* came from – through these overlapping webs of friends of friends. For me, it has to have the friendship thing, even if it's an academic or intellectual project. I remember in 2018 on the [UCU] picket line in Manchester, I realised that it's not always the person you expect. You meet people outside of your intellectual networks. I met people working on all sorts of interesting stuff, they were on the picket line in the morning, they were really nice, and they brought me a biscuit, and I'm like, I've got time for them, and so I'll go to their research seminar. And through that you're plugged in to a new set of ideas and people. That's how you find the generative and interesting connections, through forms of friendly encounter and little moments of solidarity.

Maintaining friendships can be hard though! Especially mates you can just kick about with, or mill around with. A friend recently said to me, 'do you remember being bored?' That was often with friends – unstructured time with friends. But that doesn't happen so much anymore.

Partly because, increasingly, leisure is structured by work and so for me when I think about the best kind of friendships, they're not in opposition to work. They're not defined by the fact that I'm off work.

That is what I think you're getting at with the brunch friend versus the errand friend. The harsh version of the brunch friend is that it's Instagrammable and vapid. But the more generous version is that friendship is structured by when you work. So you go for brunch because Saturday is your only free day and you want to have a drink with mates but you also don't want to stay out too late cos you've got to a do a wash and go for a run or whatever. We're diarised up to our eyeballs. So much so that going for a drink after work, even when it's not with colleagues, it's still after-work drinks. The drink or the hang-out is still defined by its relationship to work.

**Laura**: That's true. And I think that's why one of the first critiques we always get when we talk about this book is, oh friendship isn't a useful way to organise. It just doesn't have the utility of comrade, because it's either too cliquey and flawed or it's just really hard to do, especially when you're older and have to work all the time. But from what you're saying, particularly in terms of exploring political alternatives, an orientation towards friendship becomes a mode through which you live your politics.

**Luke**: Yeah, I don't understand that reproach because for me, friendship is interesting to think about because it's often not remarked on, but it is part of what makes life liveable. And everyone sort of knows that, even if they don't name it.

The type of radical friendship I'm most interested in is the type that is perhaps more evident in forms of historical struggle, that you find at a local level and that is perhaps less self-selecting. For example, migrant organising is something I always thought is really nice, because friendship in that context often says yes, we know that we might be the anarchists who believe in one thing or another or want to build a particular type of politics or whatever. But we also have to consciously build forms of humane kindness with people who we know might have different ideas. In other words, we know the negotiation is part of it. Friendship forces us to think, 'how can we talk about being kind to each other, listening to each other, changing each other, in ways that people actually do have a language for?' And friendship is a language that's very available to people.

In an earlier time, when you're thinking about organised working classes, there's a whole institutional thickness to civic life which we romanticise now but that helped to provide a context for these sorts of connections. You know, when you watch a film like *Pride*, or a Ken Loach film, there's a thickness to everyday life. There's the pub, the working man's club, the village hall, all these things. So now I'm wondering where those places might be, and how we might attend to the sort of ordinary rhythms of people's lives.

**Laura**: I think you're absolutely right that many of the spaces and institutions that encourage forms of everyday connection haven't always fared well under neoliberal-ism and our increasingly surveilled society. How does this relate to the idea of conviviality?[1]

**Luke**: There is a lot of misconceptions about conviviality. Paul Gilroy's point was never to suggest that conviviality means everyone is happy and everyone is getting along, and oh isn't it so amazing that people who are different can get along. It was actually much more about the role of difference. For example, in *After Empire* Gilroy vividly describes Guantanamo Bay, when torture and rendi-tion became very normalised with the so-called war on terror. And with all this going on you see a huge rise in anti-immigration discourse, the rise of the far right of an earlier time, of the early noughties. But what do you affirm when logics of race and nation make difference so danger-ous, when contamination and migration are made to be the problem of our time, and when whatever government we've got is hammering home this securitised, defensive kind of nationalism? Well Gilroy's response is like, actually if you just go down to the street level and go to Finsbury Park or whatever there's this thing where people don't find difference a source of danger, they don't even find it that interesting. And so conviviality is not about everyone getting along – it's about difference no longer becoming a site of danger, even when everything, politically and his-torically, is trying to force that upon us.

So we have to think about what's available and emer-gent and opening in the mass. Because the point is not to be right. The point is to work out what's going on and where the violences that we're up against – whether that's capitalist atomisation, or racism and nationalism, or male violence and patriarchy – are operating and where that is being reproduced culturally, and where that might lose its hold. And friendship is one really key lens onto what makes people want to resist, want to get involved with something, want to feel better and be better. We actually do need to look out for each other, to have food together and stuff, to build stronger ties. So it sounds cheesy to me sometimes, but it's true.

**Laura**: Maybe, then, in terms of building political movements we should be thinking – how can we create better conditions for friendship? What do we need to make friendship possible for most people? Answering that might get us closer to creating the conditions we need to make alternative politics possible. Because friendship forces us to think about third spaces, about contending with difference without creating danger, about forms of negotiation and conflict.

**Luke**: Yes, and relatedly, I think friendship is also sort of ordinary. And I guess for Gilroy, he talks about the 'radical openness' of lived culture. What nationalism and racism do, especially new racism since the Second World War, is turn culture into property that's owned by particular peoples. But I wonder if the alternative to these nationalist and racist ideas of culture is something like lived culture, and I think friendship is at the heart of that. You know like in Steve McQueen's *Small Axe* films – there's meetings and protests and parties and sex and love and arguments and

mistrust – these are beautiful representations of something *lived*.

**Laura**: Yeah. I think the ordinary livedness is really
important. And I think we can affirm that without being
prescriptive.

**Luke**: Exactly. I really like friendship because sometimes
when it comes to it, there's a kind of simplified bottom line
about what we're against and what we're for. And the point
is even if we don't know exactly what to do or how to do it,
we know that we want to retain a kind of humanity – we
want to actually *like* human beings.

**Laura**: Now I want to ask a bit about friendship and some
of the people you met as part of your work on deportation.
Your book *Deporting Black Britons* traces the life stories
of four men who have been deported from the UK to
Jamaica. So I wondered, how do people think about forms
of belonging when they are being physically dis-belonged
from places?

**Luke**: Well, for me, doing this ethnography, doing this
book, my everyday life and 'the field' are not discrete
places, and the friendships I have in 'the field' are very
real. So this makes me think about how friendship always
sits alongside other things and intersects with other parts
of life in useful ways … and not just for sociologists!
Whether that's organising a meeting, being in a union,
or interviewing someone to write up their life story for a
book – having friendship run alongside that can interrupt

it or complicate it or slow it down, and that can be confronting. But that's precisely why it's important. The idea that as an ethnographer I couldn't be friends with these people, because I'm a researcher and I'm always looking for a good story from them, yes there is an ickiness to it. But whose friendships aren't imbalanced in some way? Isn't there an ickiness when you have to work out whether you should buy your mate dinner because they've got no money? Friendships always contain imbalances, because people go through different struggles at different times. Maybe your friend is not well, or your friend has a kid and so they are a bit crap at being in touch for a while.

**Laura**: Absolutely, friendship is often about contending with power imbalances. Do you think the elasticity of friendship is what makes it so easily disregarded and demonised within the immigration system?

**Luke**: There's a particularly violent thing that happens in deportation decisions, which is that your relationships are subject to scrutiny by the Home Office, which is brutal, and in which friendship is worthless. This scrutiny exalts the nuclear familiar and codifies various forms of racist and heteronormative assumptions about other kinds of connection. The law might say well you're a parent but only a step parent, or you didn't pick your kid up from nursery enough, or in whatever way we have deemed you not significant enough in this family or whatever. This is built into immigration rules. But what if your attachment to the UK wasn't about a relationship to another person who was a partner, and it wasn't about blood or sex or

romance, and it wasn't even about fear of being perse-
cuted in the country where they are threatening to send
you. What if your argument for remaining in the UK was
simply that this is the place that you know and have come
to call home? What does it mean to say that you're socially
and culturally integrated (which is another part of the
rules)? Surely this is about friendship.

So one of the guys in the book, Ricardo, had loads of
mates that he did criminal stuff with, petty crime. But he
really did love his friends, and now they visit in Jamaica,
and a couple of them moved there. So I guess there's a way
of romanticising that – to say that Ricardo is unfairly crim-
inalised because his friends are seen as a site of dangerous
associations. And as a counter to this brutal system we
emphasise that actually friends are Ricardo's most important sites of love and connection, even if those same friends
are also part of his criminal network.

The other side of that, though, that I think is important to say, is that when I spoke with Chris [in Jamaica]
he was like, 'I don't trust anyone here.' And it's the same
if you went around in prison and asked people, 'who are
your best friends?' I guarantee loads of people will be like,
'I got a couple of real ones. But this person's fucked me
over and this person's done this or that and let me down.'
And I think that that is obviously part of how people end
up in prison.

So, yes there are all the enriching and powerful ways
that people in the deportation system have friendships
that are dismissed by the Home Office. But also so many of
them are involved in the drug economy, and what makes
life liveable for people involved in the drug economy is

whether they have friends and whether they're reliable. And well, that reality makes friendship quite important and lucrative, but also really fraught and damaging. So while we might say the youths on the street are all looking out for each other and they're mates and that's beautiful, that's only half true. They're also scared of getting stabbed. And that might mean that they don't trust their friends, or that they struggle to make friends outside of the rules of transactional violence. And so Chris saying, 'I don't trust anyone', has to be considered in the same way as Ricardo saying, 'my friends are my family'. Both men are under threat, both made to feel isolated or in danger – and friendship can be a powerful counter to that, but can also intensify it.

So you can see the friendship of people who are really up against it, and threatened in all sorts of ways, and recognise the political power of that, but at the same time acknowledge that the comfort of being in place and feeling a sense of belonging, where the friendship *isn't* embattled, is actually, maybe, the thing we really want. That what we want is for more people to have that feeling – a feeling of freedom and safety – that friendship, at its best, can absolutely provide.

**Laura**: That's a good place to end, I think. Because through this book we try to hold that tension. To say that, yes, friendship is easily romanticised, because it really is radically powerful, but also to be realistic about the ways in which friendship can be easily co-opted and can at times make the systems we fight against more effective, more harmful.

**Luke**: Yes, certainly friendship is often being commodified, emptied out, turned into something else. But it's still there, and we need it, and it opens up a space from which we can build alternatives!

# CHAPTER FIVE

# *Bad Friends*

As Luke acknowledges, friendship is complicated, but we need it! And it is politically powerful because it opens up a space from which people can imagine and enact radical transformations. Unsurprisingly, therefore, friendship is often policed as a threat. This policing happens spatially and racially, and it operates through various branches of the state apparatus and private capital. Sometimes it is implemented surreptitiously through undercover agents and shady private contracts, other times it happens in plain sight, written explicitly into policy and actualised in our urban environments. Here we highlight how attempts to curtail friendship are not new – they have been persistently and violently pursued for centuries. These dogged attempts to proscribe forms of intimacy remind us that there is something powerful in friendship. In this chapter we analyse some of the forms this policing takes, as well as think more broadly about instances of 'bad' and 'false' friendship.

We begin with an analysis of how the transformation of urban spaces has often been pursued as part of an attempt to curtail forms of revolutionary (or even just 'undesirable') sociality, both in the nineteenth century and today. We consider how this policing of urban spaces subjects certain people to more scrutiny than others, and, relatedly, how friendship is dismissed and even denigrated in the context of citizenship claims. We then turn to the history of undercover policing, focusing on nineteenth-century developments in forms of infiltration, the policing of pubs and the extensive use of *agents provocateurs*. We connect this to the far more recent 'SpyCops' scandal, in which the exposure of several undercover police officers from the Special Demonstration Squad (SDS) and the National Public Order Intelligence Unit (NPOIU) prompted an ongoing inquiry into undercover policing in Britain. We argue that the shape of political relationality in both instances was deeply affected by the presence and threat of undercover policing, but in shifting ways that reflect the historical moments being analysed. By tracing these differences, alongside certain commonalities, we can build a picture of how political organising, and the bonds of friendship that are key to this, have developed in a complex parallel to the forms of state violence used to contain, surveil and destroy them.

## SPATIAL TACTICS

Historically, as today, certain forms of gathering and socialising have been subjected to the scrutiny of the state. This is realised through various spatial tactics. In nineteenth-century Paris, for example, Haussmanisation – a vast public works programme commissioned by French Emperor Napoleon III and directed by Georges-Eugène Haussmann between 1853 and 1870 – saw the revolutionary city transformed, as its streets and neighbourhoods were replaced with wide boulevards. The working people of Paris were displaced from central districts to newly created suburbs on the peripheries to make way for luxury buildings and apartments, thus creating new geographies of separation between rich and poor. Under the guise of public health and modernisation, the principal rationale for this transformation was to curtail revolutionary assembly.

Haussmann's project of 'strategic beautification' (to use Walter Benjamin's characterisation[1]) took aim at the narrow streets of medieval Paris – sites of close-knit neighbourhood activity, known as hotbeds of unrest, and chock full of bars and cafés that served as revolutionary hangouts. The creation of the boulevards was an attempt to thwart perhaps the most iconic symbol of revolutionary Paris: the barricade. The streets targeted for destruction had frequently been barricaded by residents and revolutionaries. Between 1830 and 1848, seven armed uprisings had broken out in the centre of Paris, particularly along the Faubourg Saint-Antoine, outside the Hôtel de Ville and around Montagne Sainte-Geneviève on the left bank. The boulevards were designed to be almost impossible to barricade, while the straight lines of the new streets provided the shortest routes between military barracks and workers' districts. In short, these urban transformations were designed to physically break down the densest bonds in the city, to replace streets of furtive and friendly activity with open boulevards and squares that could be more easily surveilled and policed.

In modern Britain, the increasing transformation of public urban areas into hostile, exclusionary and privatised zones is a tactic similarly designed to discourage various forms of assembly. Anna Minton has shown how

Britain's cities have been made unfriendly, both by government intervention (or in some cases lack thereof) and by private equity and aggressive development practices.[2] For example, the Planning and Compulsory Purchase Act of 2004 made it easier for local authorities, working with developers, to compel the sale of properties on land earmarked for 'regeneration' and in the process evict people from their homes in order to build new (and generally unaffordable) developments. Crucially, this is not just an issue of housing provision – often the entire area of a regeneration zone is bought by the developer and made private, thus undermining ancient rights of way and preventing the free movement and gathering of people in these spaces. Throughout Britain, town centres and shopping arcades have been discreetly privatised in this way: 'they look at first sight like public thoroughfares, but they are run by private firms that can enforce their own social codes: no hoodies; no homeless; no protests'.[3]

Minton writes about how the use of 'defensible architecture', or hostile architecture, 'discourages strangers and diversity [and] has become the template for all new development'.[4] This urban design, then, both discourages strangers and simultaneously ensures that people remain strangers to those around them. Examples of such hostile architecture include the installation of 'anti-homeless' spikes outside flats and supermarkets, anti-skate benches, sprinklers outside buildings, high-frequency monotone sounds emitted to deter the loitering of 'youths', chlorine-filled fountains and, of course, various kinds of security camera. Many of these measures are designed to discourage anti-social behaviour, but in fact it is the impulse behind this sort of hostile urban design that is in itself anti-social, propelled by a desire to curtail forms of connection. Among the more explicit examples of policing public socialisation through architectural interventions was a series of benches installed in Cabot Square in Montreal, Canada in 2020: divided by two armrests, they also featured a Covid-inspired 15-minute time limit notice on the backrest.[5] Even more dystopian, a couple of years later Knightscope Copbots (literal robot police) began to appear in California, where they were used to monitor the presence of people gathering where they should not (particularly directed at the homeless population of San Francisco). Hostile architecture like this is often also anti-disability; it assumes that anyone lying or sitting down for prolonged periods must be up to no good.[6] While these measures are not explicitly concerned with friendship per se, they represent an expansive and expanding infrastructure designed to police people's freedom to gather, loiter, plan or protest.

Here we see how the interpersonal is a space subjected to various forms of policing. The surveillance of 'public' space, the characterisation of certain forms of assembly or intimacy as seditious, and the insidious means through which all manner of informal street life is increasingly suppressed, all constitute attempts to subdue potentially politically subversive forms of intimacy. In this context, the publicness of certain forms of friendship is what makes them so offensive to a system invested in valorising the assimilated private nuclear family as the norm. Forms of visible friendship that are hard to characterise or that might suggest 'the tying together of unforeseen lines of force' become suspicious. Such suspicions have been cod-ified in colonial settings and across British and American counterinsurgency initiatives.

As Alex Vitale argues in *The End Of Policing*, 'the police have always been political'.[7] But policing takes different forms through different configurations of political power. Early police forces were often established in Britain, Ireland and the United States in direct response to worker organising and uprisings. The London Metropolitan Police – generally regarded as the 'original' professional police force – was set up in 1829 by Sir Robert Peel, who aimed to transpose techniques he'd developed for suppressing urban uprisings in Ireland onto the English working class.

In the United States, the development of a professional police force was intimately tied to the history of slave patrols, the genocidal displacement of Indigenous people, racist border patrols, and the protection of private prop-erty for emerging urban elites. Policing techniques have repeatedly been tested on colonial populations before being deployed in colonial centres. As Arun Kundnani outlines: 'the counterinsurgency practices implemented by the British army in Malaya and in Kenya were repro-duced in Northern Ireland from the early 1970s onward', and then against racialised urban populations within Britain.[8] This reflects not only a shift in the arrangement of colonial power, but a 'periodising break' where policing is redirected towards the management of deindustrialised populations regarded as 'surplus' to capital. Mass unem-ployment, homelessness and poverty are met with mass incarceration, 'law and order' sabre rattling and the increas-ing militarisation of policing. These emerge alongside what

Kundnani and others have termed 'total policing', where the police are integrated into ever-widening 'spheres of public service provision', including education, youth services, mental health provision, housing and healthcare.[9]

We argue that the concurrent move to what we might call contemporary 'total surveillance' emerges from this context, but also from the specific ways in which undercover policing normalised the state invasion of people's personal and private lives. Undercover infiltration, and the particular techniques of false friendship encapsulated by the SDS, reflect both the historical colonial era in which they were forged and a nascent epoch of mass surveillance, mass incarceration and militarised policing. Undercover police officers made betrayal their life's work. Though there are many, many narratives of political betrayal across left-wing history, we think the more recent instances reflect contemporary state power in an important way.

Ultimately, undercover policing aims not just to infiltrate and gather intelligence on particular political groups, but to corrode the relations between group members. This too reflects the interests of those in power at any given time. As we outlined in Chapter 1, in her reading of Marx and Engels's writing on family abolition, M.E. O'Brien has demonstrated how capitalism works to destroy certain kinship ties whilst glorifying and instilling others.[10]

## FRIENDSHIP, 'THE GANG' AND THE DEPORTATION REGIME

The racist logic behind gang policing in the UK, for example, profiles public forms of alternative kinship and criminalises them. This is in part an indictment of 'the gang', which is seen to socially reproduce in ways that run counter to the successful nuclear family (gang members as wayward children with absent fathers, etc.). Joint enterprise laws make individuals complicit in their friends' crimes just by virtue of friendship, while ASBOs often stipulate who offenders can and cannot associate with, and where. Luke de Noronha has written about how, for Black boys in London, the Metropolitan police very often read their friendships through the lens of 'the gang'.[11] Moreover, 'the gang' label is not only used to secure group convictions:

> information on alleged gang-membership is now shared with local councils, housing associations, schools, and job centres. These forms of data-sharing lead to widespread discrimination and exclusion, impacting not just individuals but their families, some of whom have been threatened with evictions. Perhaps most troublingly, for those lacking British citizenship accusations of gang-membership increasingly lead to deportation.[12]

De Noronha connects the opacity of gang policing with the fear of alternative forms of social reproduction, of friendship:

> If the nation is the scaled-up counterpart to the naturalised private/nuclear family, then the reason gangs are so troubling is because they do social reproduction wrong. Unlike the nuclear family, such friendships cultivate the wrong mores and commitments, and this

explains why the criminality of 'criminal black youth' is always explained in terms of problems with the 'black family', especially in relation to 'absent fathers' – an absence which is seen to feed 'the gang'.[13]

These various forms of policing connect marginalised peoples within and across attempts to define categories of identity. Homeless people, skaters, graffiti artists, queer people, unemployed people, asylum seekers, political organisers, protesters, loiterers, dawdlers and drunks are all subject to the policing of supposedly free public spaces. There is therefore radical potential in 'the formation of new alliances and the tying together of unforeseen lines of force', that is, in *friendship*.

De Noronha's work on the spatial policing of gangs connects explicitly to the border regime. In a series of photographs titled 'No Man's Land', Nana Varveropoulou hints at the ways in which our interpersonal relationships, and our social worlds more broadly, are policed by the border regime. Varveropoulou's photographs came out of a two-year collaborative project with residents at Colnbrook immigration removal centre in Middlesex.[14] Colnbrook houses people who are at risk of deportation as they await the outcome of asylum claims or appeal deportation orders. Immigration controls have long been key sites for both the regulation of gender and sexuality and the policing of forms of intimacy. Liberal states actively define, legislate and enforce norms surrounding gender, sexuality and 'the family' at the border. Article 16(3) of the Universal Declaration of Human Rights states: 'The family is the natural and fundamental group unit of society and is entitled to protection by society and the State.' Forms of intimacy outside of this narrow nuclear frame, then, are disregarded in asylum claims and deportation appeals. People who do not socially reproduce in state-sanctioned ways, or for whom friendships constitute their closest ties, can be subject to criminalisation. The caption to one of the photos, taken by C. Gomes, hints at the disregard both for friendship ties as legal grounds for resisting deportation and for friendships made within detention facilities, where friends are frequently disappeared at short notice:

> It was very early in the morning when they came. They didn't say a word. They just said he was leaving. 'Gather your things mate' they said. He figured that he was being deported and he started screaming. Three of them took him and the rest of them gathered his things. Days later they told me he was deported. I have never heard from him since.[15]

For Gomes there is a sense of resignation about the treatment of his fellow detainee, but also a sense of loss – 'I have never heard from him since' – perhaps the loss of someone he called a friend, or just someone with whom he shared a sense of solidarity and compassion. In the photo, the wall above the bed is littered with discoloured postcard-sized squares and blu tack stains. These are a poignant reminder of all the interpersonal connections that make up a life – what mementos of connection might have been tacked to this wall by successive detainees, before being hastily taken down and tucked inside a book or a backpack at a few hours' notice?

Whatever these forms of connection, the British state has quantified, qualified, measured and judged, and in this case found them wanting: this detainee has been condemned to permanent dis-connection from the UK. This exposes a hypocrisy at the heart of the way in which the state makes decisions about people's right to belong: in many cases forms of intimacy (particularly friendship) that tie a person to Britain are deemed insufficient – they don't count. And yet when the state seeks to deport or to refuse asylum, it often does so by *emphasising* an individual's intimacy with people and places elsewhere. In this way, those seeking asylum are often characterised both as *too connected* to somewhere else (and therefore resistant to assimilation), and at the same time as lonely, aloof and suspicious. Those seeking asylum are spoken of in broad impersonal terms, and often made to appear sinister or deceitful by their mobility and perceived *lack* of ties to the place of arrival. But what if, as Anna Maguire asks, 'we saw loneliness not as something refugees are, but what they are made to be, as a form of hostility, of being inhospitable, as a weapon used by the state: to construct borders, to separate families and friends, to imprison, to detain, to deport, to take away belonging?'[16]

Friendship across categories of identity, then, might be capable of generating belonging, of producing political and interpersonal laboratories of collective action and revolutionary charge. In her classic essay, 'Punks, Bulldaggers, and Welfare Queens', Cathy Cohen argues that a radical politics needs to attend to the connections that occur across categories of identification – it should not only 'privilege the specific lived experiences of distinct communities, but also search for those interconnected sites of resistance from which we can wage broader political struggles'. She goes on: 'Only by recognizing the link between the ideological, social, political and economic marginalization of punks, bulldaggers, and welfare queens can we begin to develop political analyses and political strategies effective in confronting linked yet varied sites of power.'[17]

De Noronha's work with people awaiting deportation from Britain to Jamaica reminds us that the policing of the interpersonal is what connects people in places like Colnbrook to punks, bulldaggers and welfare queens. De Noronha talks about the cruelty of the border regime in separating families, but he is also wary about reaffirming the primacy of 'the family' – should we have to assert the ties of blood and marriage in order to make those facing deportation seem deserving? What if a deportee does not have British children or a British spouse?

Indeed, what if [their] main source of social support had been precisely those friends who the police labelled a gang? [de Noronha] met several deported people in Jamaica ... whose friendships constituted their closest ties – especially when they were younger, did not have children or monogamous partners, or were held in prisons and detention centres. This raises important questions: what is friendship worth, how might it be valued, and could it count in the context of immigration control?[18]

## FALSE FRIENDS

The policing of friendship through spatial transformations and via the border regime has contributed to long histories of clandestine networks and the creative use of public places like pubs and churches. For activists of the nineteenth century this was a defining feature of their political lives. In 1892 in the West Midlands, a group of anarchists – the so-called Walsall anarchists – were arrested on the charge of obtaining and producing explosives. They were caught in the alleged attempt to manufacture a bomb to be used against the Tsarist regime in Russia. The instigator of the plot was Auguste Coulon, a pretended anarchist and friend of several prominent activists including William Morris and Edward Carpenter. As it turned out, Coulon was in fact an *agent provocateur* employed by William Melville, a founding member of the Special Irish Branch (established to gather evidence against Fenians and anarchists) who in 1909 became the first director of the Secret Service Bureau, now known as MI5.

Coulon initiated the plot in Walsall, connecting members of the Walsall Socialist Club with contacts in Paris and London to arrange the movement of materials. The confession of one of the anarchists, Joe Deakin, exposed Coulon's role as instigator and detailed his vigorous correspondence pressing the group to prepare the bombs with increasing urgency.[19] Auguste Coulon was never arrested and was never called to testify at the trial. The same year the Walsall anarchists were arrested, the Metropolitan police raided and subsequently closed the Communard Louise Michel's internationalist school, set up in Fitzroy Square to teach children of political refugees. The closure was prompted by the discovery of explosives and bomb-making material in the building's basement, most likely placed there by Michel's friend, Auguste Coulon, who had helped to set up the school and lived on the premises.[20]

Coulon's undercover activities and the distress and suspicion they stirred in anarchist communities across Britain and beyond prompted the editor of the *Commonweal*, D.J. Nicholl, to ask, 'is it right for a political police to manufacture crime to justify its own existence?'[21] Indeed, and moreover, is it right for the state to fabricate, infiltrate and degrade bonds of friendship? How clever, and how cruel, to use friendship as a way to wreak havoc within the most intimate political spaces. And yet, how telling of the radical potential of friendship that the state would seek so determinedly to subvert and sour it.

Anarchist infiltrators like Auguste Coulon, immortalised in the fictions of Joseph Conrad and G.K. Chesterton among others, are part of the long history of undercover policing in Britain and its Empire, and of the insidious means by which the state seeks to both restrain forms of friendship and to utilise them to bolster its own power.[22] Infiltrating and fabricating friendship has long been a strategy of the state. The activities of undercover agents are not confined to the penetration of left-wing *institutions* or *formal* meetings and processes. In their pursuit of intelligence, the explicit strategies of these agents include deliberate and sustained attempts to create intimacies with activists, and to penetrate intimate and informal spaces, be they bedrooms, bathrooms or bar rooms. In other words, friendship is not a secondary or accidental consequence of the 'real' job of thwarting revolutionary activity, but is a fundamental part of such work.

Of the intimate spaces infiltrated by undercover police, perhaps the most conspicuously documented is the pub. The history of spying in pubs is as long as the history of pubs themselves. In the late eighteenth century, the London Corresponding Society, a federation of radical reading clubs set up in sympathy with the French Revolution, met regularly in pubs in central London, notably in the Globe Tavern on the Strand. When leading society members were put on trial for sedition in 1794, the prosecution relied heavily on reports of events at the Globe – including intimate dinners, toasts, speeches and individual conversations. These reports came in large part from an undercover informer. The result was the passage of the first Seditious Meetings Act (followed by a second, more punitive act passed in 1817), which took aim at the political tactics of the LCS and other working-class democratic societies. This legislation limited the number of attendees at any meeting or gathering to 50 persons, ordered prior permissions for any such meeting, and authorised justices of the peace, sheriffs and other officials to attend any meetings held within their jurisdictions. In effect, the Seditious Meetings Acts made political socialisation difficult and dangerous; they were an attack on the freedom to organise and a deliberate attempt to erode bonds of solidarity.

Nearly a century later, the pub-going proclivities of undercover agents were little changed. On any given night in the 1870s, for example, the upstairs meeting room of the

Blue Posts pub on the corner of Newman Street and East-castle Street in Fitzrovia, London, might have been host to a lecture on rent strikes or coercion in Ireland, or a meeting of land nationalisers, international socialists, exiles from the Paris Commune, or secularists, many of whom also lived and worked in the area. The pub's upstairs meeting room was dubbed the Salle des Indépendants, owing to its use as the headquarters of the French mutual assistance association, the Société des Indépendants, established by a previous generation of French émigrés in 1856. In 1871, the Salle des Indépendants became a key gathering place for exiled Communards who had escaped the wrath of the new Third Republic. The room was used by the Commu-nard's largest and most comprehensive society, La Société des Réfugiés de la Commune à Londres, which offered practical relief, comradery and political solidarity to all those who had fought for the Commune.

In the later 1870s, after the expulsion of socialists from Germany by Chancellor Otto von Bismarck, the German émigré Communist Club likewise made the upstairs of the Blue Posts its home, and members shared drinks and chat with Communards and others in the bar area. As one *London Echo* journalist put it at the time, through these intergenerational and international intimacies, revolu-tionary refugees in London created 'a veritable realisation of their pet and primary idea – *Fraternité*.'[23] In this way, friendship at the pub was political – pubs were spaces to test and enact ideas for radical futures. For political refu-gees in Fitzrovia, the Blue Posts was an informal political forum, a cosmopolitan debating society, a mutual aid association; it was a job centre, a library and a reading room. This was the intimate infrastructure of radical politics in mid and late Victorian London. And so, inevitably, endless police spies sent by foreign governments also made friends at the pub. Adolphe Smith, an English Communard who ran free English classes for political exiles in Francis Street (now Torrington Place), just off Tottenham Court Road, remembered: 'at the Blue Posts ... foreign refugees of all nationalities, and their inevitable suite of foreign police spies, indulge in continental drinks, and enjoy a few moments of leisure and chat'.[24]

The activities of these spies created cultures of suspicion within radical movements. Accusations and expulsions plagued many of the short-lived groups that sprung up around the Blue Posts in this period. The fear that friends and comrades might be working against you could undermine hard-won intimacies.

More than a century later, speaking to camera in Johanna Hamilton's 2014 documentary *1971*, John C. Raines tells of how undercover FBI policing, and the infiltration of activist groups and friendship circles active during the civil rights movements of the 1960s and '70s, similarly inculcated feelings of loneliness in those affected: 'I saw how fear within the resistance community can break the spirit of that community. That is, what happens when you begin to think "maybe she's a double agent"? That kind of thing, it shrinks the discourse. It shrinks the possibility of resistance. It makes you more lonely.'[25] Raines was a member of the Citizens' Commission to Investigate the FBI. In March 1971, Commission members broke into the FBI offices in Media, Pennsylvania and stole over 1,000 classified documents that revealed the extent of the FBI's Cold War-era illegal Counterintelligence Program (COINTELPRO). The group sent copies of the documents to all major news outlets as well as to a number of elected representatives. The leaked material exposed the Bureau's systematic use of covert surveillance, *agents provocateurs*, entrapment and illegal infiltration techniques to discredit and destroy left-wing political groups and individuals. The targets of these illegal techniques revealed the FBI's long-standing fixation with so-called un-American and civil rights groups (notably, the Black Panther Party and the anti-Vietnam war movement), and exposed the breadth of surveillance of seemingly innocuous groups and informal friendship circles.

Implicit in Raines's recollections is the sense that the FBI's methods were effective not simply because they were a means to gather information to thwart revolutionary activity, but because they undermined the fundamental *affective* bonds that activist networks rely on. They inculcated suspicion, isolation and loneliness; they threatened the very possibility of friendship.

The FBI's activities in 1960s America (and far beyond) signal the revolutionary importance of friendship. We know that friendship is integral to revolutionary organising because it is policed as a threat. As we saw earlier, the 'periodising break' of the 1970s is key here, marking a shift in how political protest was policed. In Britain, the formation of the Special Demonstration Squad in 1968 consolidated an especially paranoid and self-reproducing form of surveillance-led political policing at the heart of the London Metropolitan Police force. The SDS was instigated and managed by Special Branch, the shady collection of covert intelligence and 'counter-terrorism' units whose origins lie in the suppression of political movements in Ireland and across the British Empire. The SDS's main tactic of 'deep undercover' infiltration into thousands of political groups and movements across Britain relied on coercive techniques of befriending and relationship-building. In this way, through the constant betrayals of undercover police officers, the state built up its picture of political movements across the UK and Ireland.

## TRADECRAFT

The ongoing SpyCops hearings in Britain (officially the Undercover Policing Inquiry, or UCPI) also reveal these overlapping and emerging forms of state infiltration. Between 1968 and 2011, more than 150 undercover police officers covertly infiltrated more than 1,000 political groups in the UK, the majority of which were left-leaning. Undercover officers, as part of the SDS, engaged in a range of harmful practices including entering into sexual relationships; fathering children whilst undercover; active participation in *agent provocateur* activity; appearing in court under a false identity; and using the identities of dead children in building their false persona, without consent from families.[26] As well as the grim details of these activities, the hearings also expose the extent to which police again infiltrated and initiated friendship groups and informal pub gatherings. In 2020, Tom Foot of the *Camden New Journal* surveyed all the pubs used by activists at which undercover police officers had also gathered, forging friendships in order to observe the inti-

mate minutiae of activist life, before passing on details to
their superiors.[27] Foot's pub list is long. The reports from
the UCPI are littered with admissions from former officers explicitly acknowledging that hanging out in pubs
and forming friendships was an integral part of what
they understood their job to be. For undercover officers,
befriending activists and targets was not incidental, it was
a calculated part of their tradecraft.

The SDS was formed in 1968 after a rally against the
Vietnam War in London turned into a street battle with
the Metropolitan Police, catching them by surprise. Protesters in Grosvenor Square almost stormed the US
Embassy, causing embarrassment to the security services
and for Harold Wilson's government. A chief inspector at
Special Branch, Conrad Dixon, proposed the formation
of a new deep undercover unit aimed solely at gathering
intelligence about political groups, promising to prevent
any future outbreaks of disorder like Grosvenor. The first
book-length investigation into this era of undercover
policing, Rob Evans and Paul Lewis's *Undercover*, surveys
the history of this unit and its descendants, drawing
heavily on the testimony of whistle-blowing spy cop
Peter Francis, who infiltrated a number of anti-racist and
anti-fascist groups during the 1990s, including Anti-Fascist Action.

Francis describes one particularly infamous SDS officer,
Bob Lambert, as having the 'best SDS tour of duty ever',
between 1983 and 1988.[28] This tour included four sexual
relationships whilst undercover, fathering (and then abandoning) a child with one activist – who later described the
experience as feeling like she'd been 'raped by the state'

– and a whole range of activities aimed at subverting, disrupting and monitoring political groups. Despite, or more probably because of such activities, in 1993 Lambert was promoted to SDS operations manager. Here, he oversaw officers like Francis, who alleges Lambert told him to 'find dirt' on the family of Stephen Lawrence after his racist murder and the subsequent campaign for justice – one of at least 18 family justice campaigns the SDS also spied on during that period. Lambert then went on to head up the 'Muslim Contact Unit' at Special Branch before leaving the force in 2007 to take on academic roles at the University of St Andrews and London Metropolitan University. He was forced to resign when news about his previous undercover activities became public. In 2008 he was given an MBE for 'services to policing'.

Lambert not only acted upon but also helped codify a set of techniques to coerce people into relational bonds of trust. Here, romantic and sexual relations with women were routine, not usually for the access they gave to the particular woman being taken in, but because such relationships solidified the 'legend' (cover story) of a particular spy cop, granting them access to wider webs of friendship and connection. Lambert was one of the authors of the SDS's Tradecraft Manual, a step-by-step guide for undercover police officers that was released (though heavily redacted) as part of the ongoing SpyCops inquiry. Here was a detailed outline of how to build a 'legend', gain 'mutual trust' with people in political groups, and, crucially, how to extract yourself from these relationships at the end of a 'tour'.[29]

The UCPI documents show the monitoring of hundreds of activists in various Camden pubs (notably the Dublin Castle and the Laurel Tree) and the efforts to befriend members of the Camden branches of the Vietnam Solidarity Campaign, International Socialists and the Irish Civil Rights Solidarity Campaign, amongst others, between 1968 and 1982.[30] In the UCPI Tranche 1 Interim Report from June 2023, covering the Special Demonstration Squad (1968–82), one undercover officer, alias HN302, talks about a woman he had befriended and had sexual relations with, making it clear that the friendship was a means to bolster his cover identity:

> After a couple of meetings I developed a friendship with a woman, we had a drink ... after one of the meetings and then we went back to my [cover accommodation] ... I did not set out to sleep with anyone, but the circumstances presented themselves to me and I did not say no. Having a drink with this woman did bolster my cover identity, but the fact that we ended up having sex did not, at least in my view, provide any additional benefit in terms of cover, and that is not why I did it [but] any friendly interaction you had with anyone added layers to your legend.[31]

Beyond the personal cruelty, betrayal and callousness of the officers involved (as endemic as this was), the SDS also reflects a particular historical shift in policing and governance. While, as we have seen, undercover police officers had been using techniques of coercive sociality since their inception, the SDS represented a new phase. Here was a unit birthed through Special Branch – with its historical emphasis on 'counter-terrorism', political bombing campaigns and Irish Republicanism – and given unprecedented resources, scope and freedom to police the 'new' social movements emerging in the aftermath of 1968. Many such groups were careful about security, and organised in ways that marked a shift away from the hierarchical political party, with its membership lists, branches, elected officers and physical offices. To be clear, the SDS were also very active in older Trotskyist, labour and trade union groups that still operated in such ways, but the unit had to adapt to shifting forms of left-wing organising, with many of the most 'celebrated' officers (like Lambert) gaining renown for doing just that. While in groups like the Socialist Workers Party undercover officers could simply stand for committees or form their own (one even started his own local branch), techniques of friendship were key to embedding oneself in what became known as the New Left. Lambert's career shows how such techniques were central to the infiltration of animal rights and environmental campaigns through the 1990s and early 2000s, as part of the continual expansion of what constituted 'terrorism', 'subversion' or 'anti-state' activity.

## PATTER, PARALYSIS

It's only thanks to the tireless campaigning of groups like Police Spies Out of Lives (formed by women who were, in their own words 'deceived into intimate, sexual relationships with undercover officers'), the Undercover Research Group and Spycops.info that the practices and scale of undercover policing have been unearthed. 'Naomi', one of five women involved in the former group who went on to write *Deep Deception: The Story of the Spycop Network, by the Women who Uncovered the Shocking Truth*, makes it clear how integral coercive friendships were to undercover officers:

> Many, many people had also been close friends with Mark [undercover police officer Mark Kennedy/alias Mark Stone] so, while discussing the relationships he had, we mustn't forget the friendships these officers also betrayed. When I first met Mark, I thought we had many friends in common. It would be over a decade before I learnt that his understanding of that community, and those friendships and connections, was prior knowledge gained from other undercover cops spying on social justice networks. Spying simply for the sake of spying, to infiltrate our lives to observe us. The extent to which he would betray every one of those friendships was completely undreamt of. It seems impossible to unimagine that betrayal now, to go back to a time before that knowledge seeped into my bones, but it really never ever occurred to me then that Mark Stone was anything other than my friend.[32]

Spycops.info was started by one such deceived friend, Tom Fowler, a South Wales anarchist activist who found out that his friend and comrade in the group, 'Marco Jacobs', was an undercover police spy. In a podcast interview Fowler describes the personal toll this took on him:

I knew an undercover cop quite well, he was a close personal friend of mine ... he befriended a few of us separately [at first], and then was like 'oh you know "Michael" as well, no way!' He was funny as fuck, I have to give him credit for that, he had a whole patter – maybe he was just tuned into my humour on purpose, but he was funny.[33]

Jacobs cultivated a 'blokiness' and an opaque working-class history (posing as a truck driver to justify extended periods of time spent back in his real life) that also centred around heavy drinking, pubs and the social centre and party scene. As another activist, 'Verity Smith', recounts: 'He would be down the pub all the time, he would always have money for drinks, he would be very keen to encourage people to go out drinking with him and used that time to really probe people on what they thought and what their attitudes were and what their opinions were, what their vulnerabilities were.'[34] Jacobs was also, in Fowler's terms, 'a massive fucking gossip', raking over people's private and personal details and 'exhausting people with internal bullshit'. Such tactics were common among undercover officers, always aiming at embeddedness and disruption. The aforementioned SDS Tradecraft Manual detailed different tactics for gaining 'mutual trust', ranging from getting embedded in a new locality – 'Visit the local entertainment (be it a pub, cinema, swimming pool or ice rink) or whatever else you feel is a necessary part of becoming a real person in your new home' – to what the guide sickeningly calls 'the thorny issue of romantic entanglements'.[35] Jacobs engaged in both, and Fowler describes the aftermath of all this in both personal and political terms: 'I was completely paralysed [politically] for years to be honest. And on a wider level, that goes for society at large – what kind of society would Britain be without the SpyCops? ... these units were designed to undermine democracy on an industrial scale.'[36]

Fowler imagines a counterfactual left-wing British history where the miners' strike, trade unions and a whole range of environmental, anarchist, animal rights, anti-racist and socialist movements had not been spied upon and disrupted from inside. This sense of temporal disjuncture has a personal edge too: 'I feel like I'm stuck in a time-loop of being 25 to 30, because that's how old I was when it happened. And I've over-analysed those five years of my life in a way which is not healthy, and I have no desire to do, but I know there is this log of every fucking move I made during that time. 50,000 documents or some crazy shit, just on me.'[37] Here we find a cruel inversion of the 'personal is political' played out in the form of state violence. As 'Alison', another of the authors of *Deep Deception*, puts it:

Our stories illustrate, in the most concrete way, the feminist adage: the personal is political. While it's our personal stories that have generated the most public awareness of the Metropolitan Police's actions, it's essential to us that their political dimension is not lost. What happened to women like us is central to how the police functioned. The exploitation and abuse of women was fundamental to the undercover officers' success in the field.[38]

In Fowler's words: 'These are undercover political police, but they are not doing political infiltration, they are doing personal infiltration. They infiltrate people's personal lives and by the means of being inside people's personal lives, they spy on political movements ... The effectiveness of the deployment is based upon how much you mess with people's personal lives.'[39]

The acute sense of betrayal, anger and paralysis was shared by many people Fowler got to know as the SpyCops' revelations gathered pace: 'for a lot of people, they've never done politics again since ... I mean I was lucky, I was only considered a mad conspiracy theorist for a few months, before it was on the front page of *The Guardian*. But other people had been doing it [trying to investigate suspected undercover cops] for decades.' Conversely though, it was through these very connections, and collective work to expose undercover policing in Britain, that Fowler was able to re-enter political work and re-establish relations of comradely trust. As he explains: 'knowing so many of the women who've been affected and having those people as my close friends and comrades has been incredibly inspiring. ... this has defined their lives in a way that they are not willing to let slip, they are not going to let it go. Its something we've all got in common when we are dealing with this, we've all got to keep turning up.'[40]

Or as 'Alison' puts it:

In spite of the horrendous nature of what's happened, I'm buoyed by the camaraderie and comradeship I've had the opportunity to experience as a consequence of it all. Groups and individuals from different backgrounds and political traditions have succeeded in working together to expose this wrongdoing. Together, we are a formidable force and I hope that fact gives these officers and their managers regular nightmares.[41]

## FALL GUYS

The inquiry into undercover policing has moved at a laborious pace, as the volume of evidence continues to mount. Originally announced by then Home Secretary Theresa May in 2015, as of July 2024 the inquiry had only reached 'Tranche 2' of five, focused on SDS activity between 1983 and 1992. It is difficult therefore to know how these practices shifted in more recent times. The SDS and its successor, the National Public Order Intelligence Unit (NPOIU), formed in 1999, no longer exist. The latter was merged into the National Domestic Extremism Unit in 2010. No doubt contemporary police infiltration draws heavily on the ubiquity of smartphones, CCTV and digital surveillance, along with older practices of recruiting 'confidential informants' (CIs), and an increased range of privatised surveillance, blacklisting and spying services. The specific forms of coercive relationality practised by the SDS and NPOIU may be less necessary in such a context. They may also be less affordable, under the conditions of austerity that informed May's decision to investigate a police force she was attempting to cut back.

At a deeper level of police culture and management personnel, however, there is little doubt that the ethics and practices of units like the SDS have informed policing in Britain in profound ways. The sense of entitlement to pry into people's personal lives, the disregard for their privacy, and the paranoid view of what constitutes 'subversion' that was honed and codified by the SDS have had far wider reach. Remember that figures like Bob Lambert, co-author of the SDS Tradecraft Manual, went on to spend many years in positions of management and influence within the police and academia. A telling Appendix in the SDS manual gives a 'view from the street' written by a 'field officer' (possibly Lambert or his mentee Francis) that captures the paranoia, entitlement and angry authoritarianism of such figures:

> The police always appear as the fall guys or aunt sally's. This is because of lack of decisive action and leadership. Most of this could be avoided if we lose the notion of it will look bad if we appear to be moving toward a paramilitary force. ...

> It is difficult to portray the intense hatred of the police felt by most of the aforementioned groups [Anti-Fascist Action, anarchists, Red Action, the 'extreme left']. When the conditions are right the demonstrators will unite into a maelstrom of violence directed against the police which is virtually impossible to contain or control. ...

> I believe that riot police ready and available on site will deter 85–90% of potential trouble makers. So why be afraid to deploy them like that from the start? The reason is usually incompetence and cowardice on the part of senior management.[42]

Here we see the seeds of a particular vision of draconian policing – forged in the heat of a coercive undercover policing 'tour' – that has only gathered pace since the formal disbanding of units like the SDS. Across areas of protest policing, data protection, state surveillance and 'counter extremism' (most visibly through the Islamophobic and deeply invasive Prevent Duty), successive governments have repeatedly acted to impede personal liberty, privacy and the right to protest. The most recent apotheosis of this, the 2022 Police, Crime, Sentencing and Courts Act, involved a huge clampdown on protest, sweeping new police powers and the criminalisation of Gypsy, Roma and Traveller communities. The widespread resistance to this, in the form of the #KillTheBill protests, served as a reminder of just how unashamedly 'paramilitary' the contemporary British police now are, with many protestors beaten by cops and heavily sentenced because of their involvement. The 2022 Acts' follow up, the Public Order Act 2023, then introduced Serious Disruption Prevention Orders (to prevent or prohibit people from participating in protest), increased stop and search powers and new protest offences.

It is in this climate that we are seeing record sentences for nonviolent protest, including five Just Stop Oil protestors being sentenced to between four and five-and-a-half years in jail for 'conspiracy to cause a public nuisance' in July 2024, after speaking on a Zoom call about recruiting volunteers for an action that would have blocked the M25 motorway.[43] Similarly, six people from the Palestine Action protest group were detained in August 2024 under the Terrorism Act, after taking direct action against the

Israeli-owned Elbit arms factory in Bristol. Such draconian measures may suggest the obsolescence of the deep undercover tactics employed by the SDS and NPOIU, but this is not guaranteed. What is certain is that the detailed picture of 'political groups' painted by hundreds of undercover police over the last decades (in 2013 the England and Wales police watchdog admitted to having 1,229 officers across 39 units at that point[44]) has percolated across the police in profound ways. These views emerged from codified relations of coercive friendship and mendacious romantic entanglement, with all the guilt and paranoia they involve.

As this chapter has shown, the state's capacity and sense of entitlement to police and surveil our relational lives has only increased since the SDS was founded in 1968. Historic tactics for policing space and colonised populations have been reconfigured into new iterations of draconian surveillance and control. It's hard to estimate the impact that state infiltration has had on left-wing movements, protest groups and trade unions in Britain, forcing us to adapt to doing political work in a climate of suspicion, uncertainty and fear. The spectre of the false friend seeps into everyday political life in ways far wider than the reach of any one spy cop. As Tom Fowler and the women behind Police Spies Out of Lives demonstrate, perhaps one of the only ways out of this bind is (counterintuitively?) to dig deeper into bonds of real friendship. Bad and false friends, for all the pain and trauma they inflict, can illuminate the operation of state power, showing how 'dense bonds' are deeply threatening to its operation. Rebuilding these in the face of betrayal is not easy, but we can take inspiration from those who have managed to do this, despite unimaginable personal deception. As Sita Balani writes, the defiant responses of people who have spoken out about their experiences of spy cops, like Tom Fowler, the McLibel activist Helen Steel and many others, 'form an extraordinary archive. A counternarrative to Special Branch's surveillance. It includes evidence of all sorts of other intimacies – those built up between campaigners in meetings, on demonstrations, painting banners, and strategizing together – forged in the teeth of covert political surveillance.'[45]

The last word for now to 'Lisa', in *Deep Deception*, who shares an email she sent to her former partner 'Mark Stone' after he pleaded with her for forgiveness in the aftermath of being outed as a spy cop:

Date: Wed, 3 Nov 2010, 19:06

I'm not sure I can begin to know what to say! A bomb has exploded in my life, blowing it apart and also affecting dozens and dozens of amazing people who considered you a friend. Quite frankly I'm still numb with shock. ...

I'm afraid there's no fairy-tale ending to this story. You might have thought you were living life in a film script, being the exciting double agent, but I'm sorry you don't get to run off with the girl in the end.

I'm being shown such a huge amount of fiercely true love from so many incredible people that I can't let down.

I choose them.[46]

# CHAPTER SIX

## Friends in Common

### A BAND ON EVERY BLOCK

Watching *We Jam Econo: The Story of the Minutemen*, on YouTube, lying in bed. The film is grainy, a bit all over place, and emotionally moving, much like the band it profiles. Early on, bass player Mike Watt walks around the park where he first met guitarist and singer D Boon, his future best friend and bandmate. 'I met D Boon when I was 13 and we were playing and he fell out of a tree onto me', explains Watt. 'This is the tree', he says, holding onto a branch as he chats through the pair's early days of hanging out, jamming and listening to records: 'I was quite smitten with him.' The two went on to form the kind of deep, supportive friendship that can let creativity and weirdness flourish, forging a whole musical, ethical and political world from the garages of their working-class San Pedro neighbourhood, on the outskirts of Los Angeles.

Boon died aged 27 in 1985 in a freak van accident, marking the end of the Minutemen, one of the most singular punk bands of the 1980s. Filmed in 2005, *We Jam Econo* sees Watt still working through the grief of this loss, driving round San Pedro, reflecting on what the band meant to him. With music that drew on post-punk, country, jazz, rock and folk, the Minutemen are perhaps just as well known for their DIY working-class ethos of 'we jam econo': doing things at low cost and making shows affordable and accessible to ordinary people from their community. The film uses various bits of archived footage of the band filmed before Boon's death; in one interview he speaks about 'econo' with typical gusto: 'There should be more interaction with music and everyday people ... We want people to know, there should be a band on every block, there should be a nightclub on every other block and a record label on every block after that.'[1]

Often writing songs about their own struggles with shit bosses and hard jobs, the band lived the ethos of 'rise with your class, not above it', playing early evening shows that meant people with work the next day could attend more easily, keeping ticket prices as low as possible, learning to fix their own vans and gear, and encouraging every-one to start their own bands too. On their classic album *Double Nickels on the Dime* the band reference James Joyce, Marxism and anti-imperialism, protesting every-thing from crap TV adverts to the legacy of the Vietnam war. As the writer Stewart Smith outlines in a 40th anni-versary celebration of the album:

An avid reader of history and politics, Boon was under no illusions about the trail of death and destruction left by the US in the name of anti-communism, from South East Asia to South America ... 'Untitled Song For Latin America' addresses Reagan's funding of right-wing paramilitaries in Nicaragua, Guatemala and El Salvador. A member of the Committee in Solidarity with the People of El Salvador, Boon pulls no punches: 'The western hemisphere and all inside/ We know who's murdering the innocent ... I would call it genocide/ Any other word would be a lie'. Heard today, the song is all too relevant.[2]

Political commitment did not mean earnest or didactic sermonising though; the album also rips through self-deprecating jokes – 'We were fucking corndogs/ We'd go drink and pogo' – irreverent musical history and scat humour (track 27 of 45: 'The Roar Of The Masses Could Be Farts'). Enduring through all of this is a sense of locality and intimacy that emanates from the profound, if often quarrelsome, friendship between Boon and Watt. Yet this is a locality that reaches out, that imagines multiple interlocking bands, scenes and ways of doing music – connected through a shared openness and opposition to elite, corporate culture. Crucially, it also contextualises this within histories of colonial and capitalist violence, linking them back to people's everyday experiences, and encouraging them to reflect creatively on these.

Contrast this to the dominant form of 'locality' we see today, in which local markers, words and symbols are turned into branding devices for municipal government and businesses to drive gentrification and attempt to paper over the cracks of a largely decimated urban and public landscape. In Glasgow, the City Council led 'rebranding' exercises such as the 1980s 'Glasgow's Miles Better' campaign (featuring a beaming cartoon Mr Happy) and the more recent 'People Make Glasgow' slogan coincide with a gift-shop avalanche of tea-towels, hats and riso-printed posters covered in 'bampots', 'bawbags', 'ayes' and trendily rendered paintings of favourite local businesses.

The working-class history of the city is both captured and erased in such instances, offering a culturally capitalised vision of community rather than encouraging practices of actual community building. The 'authentic' and 'local' here is specific enough to be marketised while being actually endlessly replicable: in Newcastle you'll find 'Howay man' and 'Alreet Pet', in Bristol 'Gert Lush' and 'Alright my Luvver'; the list goes on. Locality becomes a brand to fit oneself within, just one of many contrasting but somehow similarly bland flavours, rather than a scale from which to organise and make connections. As the geographer David A. Banks argues, in this realm of what he calls *The City Authentic*, 'cities are encouraged by governments and businesses to act like reality TV stars and social media influencers – to become cartoons of themselves' as the nostalgic branding of urban areas masks structural disinvestment and 'gives rise to a ravenous real estate market that mines the delicate patina of history for profit'.[3] This coincides with the removal and racialised policing of spaces of friendship that we outlined in the last chapter: youth clubs closed, music venues shut and wider public spaces walled off and patrolled. Instead of the kind of interconnected, mutually supportive and wildly different scenes we find in the ethos of the Minutemen, here we see locality and community as supplantable and contained.

\* \* \*

But what might it mean to think differently about the relationship between friendship and community at different scales? Is it possible to make localised and interpersonal friendships matter for much broader political transformation? Can friendship overlap with solidarity and ideas of 'the commons'?

In this chapter we argue that combining friendship, solidarity and 'the commons' is not only possible, but necessary, and that it relies on acknowledging and building upon the already existing ways in which 'local' and 'global' movements are interconnected. As we argue, this means avoiding the unidirectional and universalising motions of coercive 'friendship' we see in both colonial encounters and flattened notions of solidarity. It means thinking about the modes of communication we can build to speak across differences, to see the mutuality and productive tensions that emerge across divergent struggles. It also means finding the physical spaces – never reducible to a sanitised 'People Make Glasgow' vision of locality – where friendship and political struggle can feel tangible and powerful, and using this to connect this to movements in different times and places. It might be a DIY venue, a protest kitchen, a community archive, a queer sauna or a public square. Such spaces, at their best, don't simply contain 'community' but question the terms of access to it, along with the distribution of resources and capital that condition our sociality, always already infused with overlapping forms of the 'global' and 'local'.

Both physical and digital space can demonstrate the importance of cultivating mutual critique and shared boundaries of access, along with how friendship can help us discern these difficult processes. In a Bluesky thread about what it means to disagree solidaristically in online debate, M.E O'Brien quotes a 1970 speech by the Black

Panther leader Huey P. Newton: 'Friends are allowed to make mistakes. The enemy is not allowed to make mistakes because his whole existence is a mistake, and we suffer from it. But the women's liberation front and gay liberation front are our friends, they are our potential allies, and we need as many allies as possible.'[4] As O'Brien goes on to argue, 'where we draw the line between enemies and potential allies is a central question of politics, and is always debatable'.[5] Practices of everyday solidarity and friendship help illuminate how we might draw this line, along with the ways in which coalition building necessarily involves disagreement, antagonism and discomfort. Such an initiative, as we saw in Gracie and Gargi's respective evocations of 'fellow travellers' and 'comradely letter writing', does not necessitate imposing flattened ideas of 'left unity', but requires generating different ways of sharing ideas, debating strategy and acknowledging points of departure. This is the work of solidarity, and of embedding relations of 'everyday solidarity' into our lives.

As Lola Olufemi admits, 'solidarity is hard to define', but she offers some rich suggestions: 'working across difference, standing together in the face of shared oppression and standing alongside those with whom you do not share common experience of the world'. She also argues that 'at the core of solidarity is mutual aid: the idea that we give our platforms, resources, legitimacy, voices, skills to one another to try and defeat oppressive conditions'.[6] Solidarity is an outlook and process, then, as well as a feeling. It involves reflection, material redistribution and humility, along with the possibility of transforming those who practise it. In a 2018 blog post titled 'Notes Towards a Theory of Solidarity', written as part of a UCU strike teach-out, the writer Jeremy Gilbert argues that solidarity is 'never primarily about shared *identities* but about shared *interests*', not just in terms of key demands and shared material needs, but in the sense of the commonality and personal transformation that solidarity can engender.[7]

Such sentiments echo writing on the idea of solidarity by the poet Denise Riley, who makes it clear that 'it's hard enough to be solid in myself'.[8] Here we see how 'identities may first have to be loosened or laid aside for the sake of solidarity',[9] as the recourse to 'we' changes that which it holds together: it 'names new subjects different from the old selves which enunciate them'.[10] Solidarity changes that which coheres through it, as well as pointing to the way any previously presumed solidity or boundedness is also illusory. As Olufemi argues, political 'movements have always been attuned to one another', and 'solidarity breaks down the concept of the nation or the idea that the world and the many countries it contains are not linked by present and historical networks of exploitation, colonial rule and military alliances'.[11] Solidarity highlights our interconnection, and asks us to act upon this.

This chapter connects questions of locality and internationality to these ideas of solidarity, building an argument about the role of friendship through all this. Put simply: expressions of solidarity often rely upon everyday experiences of friendship. Harry Blatterer argues that 'friendship, as instantiation of intimacy and site of moral learning, is conducive to solidarity understood as felt concern for unknown others'.[12] He considers how the practice of friendship helps to connect private and public, or, to put it another way, to connect the interpersonal with the societal so that friendship might 'help us understand the meaning and evaluate the quality of solidarity not only cognitively and abstractly but emotionally and concretely – comprehensively'.[13] Beyond its contribution to individual friends, then, friendship's intimacy, perhaps counterintuitively, 'bridges the divide between the private and public domains in societies of strangers'.[14] This is where we find its power – friendship connects big and small ideas, it leaks out from the personal into the social, and it can connect the hyperlocal and the international.

Acts of solidarity require an effort of imagination to empathise with the struggle of another, as well as inhabit a sense of shared possibility in addressing this. Such acts rely on a capacity to feel and experience that effort through actual experiences of intimacy and connection. And this relies on friendship.

## A UNIVERSAL LANGUAGE OF FRIENDSHIP?

In attempting to think through the broader implications of friendship, we cannot simply abstract its key impulses, deploy them indiscriminately and expect a stock outcome. Indeed, a dangerously vague universal idea of friendship has been forever used to justify imperial expansion, exploitive and extractive relationships and the subjugation of peoples. 'Friendship' between countries often signals trade agreements, quid pro quos and geopolitical decisions made underhand and over handshakes. As Alecia Simmonds demonstrates in her study of friendship and colonialism, the eighteenth century is often characterised as a period that witnessed the 'liberation of friendship from the instrumentalist bonds of the market, creating a voluntarist, sentimental and private relationship'. When harnessed to imperial ambition, however, 'friendship appears in an almost diametrically opposite form: coercive, commercial, and public'.[15]

In an imperial context, the language of friendship has been a coercive means of colonialism, resting upon an idea, drawn from Roman law, of sociable global trade. Enlightenment ideology enabled the ruling naval elite of the eighteenth century to consider their invasions friendly, despite the manifest violence of colonial occupation.[16] For example, the instructions issued to Captain James Cook on his first voyage on *HMS Endeavour* to Tahiti, New Zealand and Australia from 1768 to 1771 advised captains to 'observe the Genius, Temper and Inclinations or Dispositions of the natives and to endeavour by all proper means to cultivate a Friendship and Alliance with them'.[17] Similarly, when British naval officers arrived in Botany Bay, Australia in 1788, to create the penal colony that would become the first British settlement in Australia, they depicted their interactions with the Eora people as friendly and declared sympathy towards them. 'This sympathetic friendship enabled them to violently impose their culture while maintaining the self-perception that they were polite, enlightened gentlemen bringing the gift of civilization.'[18] The refusal of that friendship by the Eora reinforced the idea that they lacked sociability and sympathy. In this context, 'the officer's performance of polite friendship became a reiterative practice of racialized discourse whereby the inner virtues of sympathy and manly self-control were embodied as white and simultaneously denied to the Eora in their current culture'.[19]

These imperial visions of 'friendly' violation and destruction show how figurative friendship can be stretched beyond all meaning, abstracted into something so bombastic as to become almost completely untethered from individual commitments, integrity and feeling. Or else friendship is relegated and made entirely personal, private, apolitical. Friendship, then, or at least many of the ways in which people have named it, is often at once too vast and too narrow to be of any real generative consequence.

In centring friendship this book has reanimated the ways in which the radical *practice* of friendship can have revolutionary potential, precisely because it can bridge the small and the big, the personal and the collective. Friendship is about individuals, and it relies on a sense of intimacy, closeness and care, but it is also capable of connecting struggles across time and place, to world-bending effect. E.M. Forster famously said that if he 'had to choose between betraying my country and betraying my friend, I hope I should have the guts to betray my country'.[20] Forster was writing in 1938 just as Adolf Hitler, Neville Chamberlain, Édouard Daladier and Benito Mussolini were hashing out the details of the Munich Agreement, and the drumbeat of European nationalism was again utilising the language of friendship in service of a kind of white civility, again with dire and violent consequences. Forster's defiant defence of the friend points to the revolutionary potential of friendship. In his epigram there is the suggestion that to define ourselves by and organise our lives around friendship, rather than attach ourselves unquestioningly to a cause or a creed, is our best hope. 'Personal relationships', he writes, 'here is something comparatively solid in a world full of violence and cruelty'.[21] Friendship keeps the individual in view, and only by doing so can we resist the dehumanising narratives of race and nation. Understood this way friendship contains within it the potential to resist the state and to challenge assigned hierarchies of allegiance: 'Love and loyalty to an individual can run counter to the claims of the State. When they do – down with the State, say I.'[22] This direct link between affective structures in the smallness of our day-to-day lives and political actions and movements capable of upending massive structures of power is what makes friendship so vital.

## FRIENDSHIP AS A MILITANT PARTICULARISM

Friendship can clearly be deployed in nationalist and colonial processes then, along with resistances to them. Raymond Williams's concept of 'militant particularisms' is useful here in considering ways of understanding the relationship between specificity and generality. Coined by Williams on the basis of his observations of communities in South Wales, the concept was developed by David Harvey to refer to the particularist origins of struggle. Harvey takes Williams' phrase to mean that politics is always embedded in 'ways of life' and 'structures of feeling' peculiar to particular places and communities, and thus always bears the mark of this specificity and situatedness, both in terms of the issues at stake and the tactics and imaginaries deployed.[23] In his study of labour relations at the Cowley motor works in Oxford, Harvey interpreted Williams's model as implying a dichotomy between local and global, experiential and abstract, place and space. A militant particularism, then, might be a conflict between a local landowner and a group of workers seeking to graze animals: a conflict in a particular place and at a particular time over a particular issue. Harvey suggests that while, for example, 'the socialist cause in Britain has always been powered by militant particularisms', they can only get us so far. By themselves, they are often too rooted and bounded to reach out-of-place and across space. He asks how we might develop or scale up these local, everyday solidarities into universal political imaginaries capable of producing much larger structural change. Friendship, too, is often conceptualised in this way, as something nourishing and affirming for an individual – important in developing ideas and identities, but somewhat trivial and not really up to the task of changing structures or crafting doctrine, or reaching the global heights of its much more expansive big sister, international solidarity.

In the conclusion of *The Rentier City*, Isaac Rose quotes Harvey's reading of Williams's concept in order to ask how militant particularisms such as the 'Block the Block' neighbourhood campaign in Manchester might be 'generalised and universalised' to meet the challenge of aggressive capitalist development more generally. In Harvey's words: 'the move from tangible solidarities understood as patterns of social life organised in affective and knowable communities to a more abstract set of conceptions that would have universal purchase involves a move from one level of abstraction – attached to place – to another level of abstraction capable of reaching out across space'.[24]

As Rose goes on to point out, Harvey never quite gives us an answer as to how this move might be made. But perhaps the very framing of the problem is wrong. In it Harvey sets up a binary between the knowable, limited and local and the abstract, connected and global. Like the influential 'Post-Marxist' philosophers Michael Hardt and Antonio Negri, Harvey demands that any alternative to neoliberal globalisation be global in scale, since adopting strategies of local resistance 'misidentifies and thus masks the enemy'.[25] This is misleading, and suggests that these scales do not overlap or interact. Katrina Navickas, writing about protest and contestation over the right to use public space in North West England during the Age of Revolution, contests Harvey's interpretation of militant particularisms. She argues that the women and men who marched on Lancashire moorlands in an effort to claim their right to meet and speak there were not parochial in their aims. They were certainly invested in their locale but they were part of much broader and connected struggles against processes of enclosure everywhere: 'Although custom, local rights and exclusion were crucial layers forming the palimpsest of place ... a search for a wider class identity and solidarity could co-exist with a defence of place'.[26] In other words, we might understand the aforementioned local conflict between a landowner and a group of workers wishing to graze animals, 'not [as] local protectionism but [as] a critique of dispossession', as Doreen Massey puts it.[27]

More fundamentally even, Harvey's construction of place versus space, local versus global, obscures the connections that already constitute 'the local'. These localised conflicts are the ongoing products of the diverse routes and connections that make up spaces of struggle. In other words, the 'local' in all of these constructions is never entirely local to begin with anyway; as Massey notes elsewhere, places 'are always constructed out of articulations of social relations ... which are not only internal to that locale but which link them to elsewhere. Their "local uniqueness" is always already a product in part of "global" forces, where global in this context refers not necessarily to the planetary scale, but the geographical beyond, the world beyond the place itself.'[28] Perhaps then, as Paul Gilroy (via James Clifford) encouraged, when thinking about histories of struggle we would be better served by thinking about 'routes' rather than 'roots'.[29]

The representation of militant particularisms as thoroughly rooted is not only misleading but can also have damaging consequences. For example, the Luddites explored in Chapter 2 were very much invested in their local circumstances and landscapes, and their alliances were forged through networks of friends and neighbours. Some scholars have, therefore, resurrected the Luddites in service of a bounded, traditional localism. Kirkpatrick Sale, for example, uses them to argue for a rehabilitation of 'the tribal mode of existence ... consonant with the true underlying needs of the human creature',[30] suggesting that this traditional, pre-industrial 'strategy of localism' is the Luddites' greatest legacy.[31] In doing so Sale reifies the 'primitive' in the local; he makes Luddite politics romantic, static and essentialist. In David Featherstone's words, '[Sale] threatens to make radical environmental politics a politics against any kind of future rather than one with a horizon which actively engages with emergent histories and geographies.'[32]

This construction of histories of radicalism as bounded can lend itself to forms of cultural nationalism that exclude subaltern forms of struggle and organising. For Massey, the 'popular past was not the inward-looking bounded localism so often counterposed to an equally erroneous vision of a present that is globally open'.[33] All the radical movements we have explored here – swing rioters in Buckinghamshire, Parisian Communards, activists in Rojava, bands writing music in basements in 1980s suburbia – were acting in the context of wider connections, influences and debates. Confining forms of struggle to a static place-bound 'local' reifies the idea that only fully intellectualised and globalised movements, guided by robust political theory (generally of the Western Enlightenment variety), can hope to bring about real transformation. Indeed, while there is a wealth of scholarship on radical resistance to modern empire and the ways in which colonial subjects took up Western ideas and turned them against empire – 'striking back' to make claims to freedom and self-determination – these works often continue to present only a one-directional flow *from* centre *to* periphery, from metropole to subaltern, from the West to the rest.

Reversing this flow, Priyamvada Gopal asks instead, 'what if we explored the possibility that Britain's enslaved and colonial subjects were not merely victims of this nation's imperial history and subsequent beneficiaries of its crises of conscience, but rather agents whose resistance not only contributed to their own liberation but also put pressure on and reshaped some British ideas about freedom and who could be free?'[34] In other words, international movements, big political ideas and broad-based resistance movements are made through multiplicities: through connections, through everyday struggle, through friendship and community, through localised action across various scales in various places. Featherstone uses the example of the solidarity shown by Lancashire cotton workers for the anti-slavery movements in the United States in the 1860s (which influenced the intellectual development of Karl Marx) to demonstrate that 'these connections and solidarities were … not produced by dispassionate elites; they were forged through the actions of dispossessed workers who had much to gain in the short term by breaking the cotton blockade'.[35] In short, radical resistance has always been animated by relational connections and the development of friendships and everyday solidarities. Therefore,

> it is empirically incorrect, and politically a cul-de-sac, to counterpose a bounded localism against an ungrounded, disembedded globalism. Neither can be the basis for a future on different terms. A real internationalism in the political sense might better stem from a recognition of the multiplicity of local specificities, but where such specificities are themselves open to the wider world.[36]

So what does this mean for friendship? Navickas's and Featherstone's insistence that local place-based activity need not exist in opposition to broad political identities might be a useful way to think about friendship. In other words, it might help us to think about the relationship between individual friendships and friendship as a way of life, friendship as an important part of a much broader political identity: friends in common. Rather than thinking about anti-capitalist struggle as a universally experienced and articulated idea, could we instead think of it as a connected and relational series of trans-local friendships, where the local might be attached to a place, or to a person, without being bound by that locality? If individual friendship makes us alive to intimacies, conflict, power dynamics and contestation, could we understand true internationalist solidarity to mean a multiplicity of all these friendships? Thought about this way, we could say that friendship itself is a militant particularism; friendship is not formed and *then* networked: wherever we find it, it is already itself a product of ongoing networks and relational processes which are connected through space to friendships and solidarities elsewhere.

Histories of friendship, like some of those discussed in this book, are, then, in themselves a way of multiplying connection; they help us discover the routes (past and future) of everyday solidarities. These friendships are not universal or abstract: they are made and lived in-place, but, as expressions of an aspiration for connection and community, they *can* reach out across time and space.

## FRIENDS IN COMMON

What does it mean then, to be in common? We called this book *Friends in Common* partly because that's how we met

– through a friend in common – but also because for us the phrase speaks to friendship beyond proximate inter-personal intimacy. It signals 'dense bonds' as modes of belonging that can encompass anonymous, fleeting affin-ity and deeply enmeshed personhood. We also intended the title to be a nod to the commons, to the process of commoning, of holding things *in common*. As the anthro-pologist Miriam Ticktin outlines:

> The commons has come to mean many things (and is practised by many different people, from indigenous communities to Black and Brown communities, to ecologists to anarchists), but it is often referred to as a struggle against enclosures, the privatization of spaces of freedom, exclusion, and, perhaps most importantly, private property. It can also mean the sharing of wealth and resources on the basis of collective decision-mak-ing; sometimes it is spoken of as grounded in social relations built on reciprocity, respect, mutuality, and responsibility.[37]

We chose not to start this book with 'what we all have in common' though, as tempting as such rhetoric often is. Instead, we hope that the assortment of ideas assembled here points a different way towards 'commonality', not as intrinsic or universal but as emerging through struggle and discussion, always in process. The history of the Euro-pean and US left is littered with examples of unilateral declarations of solidarity and evocations of a collective 'we', of an assumed 'common ground' that dampens the possibilities for genuine coalition work and self-reflection.

This idea emerges in dialogue with an ahistorical notion of the commons, and of common land in particular, that has been endlessly romanticised, imagined as a utopian space, open to all.

In fact, the commons of the past were never intrinsically free for all to use. Common land was never *owned* by commoners, it was owned by the lord of the manor, the aristocrats, but it could be communally used and legally accessed for particular purposes. The rights of use of the commons were not universal: the commons has always been made through a patchwork of customary rights, shifting agreements and knotty negotiations. These negotiations could be fraught with jealousy and scheming, and the privatisation and commercialisation of common rights has been ongoing since at least the seventeenth century. Indeed, some forms of enclosure were enacted or encouraged by commoners themselves in order to broker more lucrative deals with landowners or other commoners. Importantly, though, the process of commoning was determined by the people involved, the people for whom the commons meant something, rather than by the application of a rigid set of principles prescribed from a far-off place.

Enclosure, then, is the removal of this common right to use the land, and it comes in various forms. In Britain, the enclosure of the commons accelerated in the eighteenth century, but it was a much longer process stretching back to the thirteenth century, and it continues today. Gradually, through a combination of legal decrees, private acts and bureaucratic processes, huge amounts of land across Britain moved from a system of shared open fields (with no hedges or fences) to a system of enclosed private farms. This process has been consistently and ferociously challenged throughout its long history. As Ticktin outlines, the commons should be understood as sites of *struggle against* enclosure. The fierce protests that people enacted and the radical activities they pursued to resist enclosure are where we find the real allure of the commons. In other words, the commons represents long histories of connected struggle and the imaginative possibilities that these histories continue to generate.

Perhaps, then, we can find in the commons something like the logic of friendship: it is not automatically open to all, but nor does it automatically prescribe criteria via which to exclude or enclose. Friendship is predicated on relationality, on negotiation. It is always in process, always changing; it cannot be prescriptive or universal. But therein lies precisely its power. Many of our present-day democratic ideas have been built instead on an ideal of a *universal* public protected by a set of universal principles guaranteeing justice and fairness, and yet the reality many of us experience is the converse – a closing down of openness, vicious individualism and dangerous practices of exclusion.

This raises questions we would need to come back to. What would it mean to 're-common' land, space and resources for mutual and shared use? How might this apply to a 'digital commons' and the other spaces of discussion and meeting that political life requires? What can we learn about creating the conditions for friendship and anti-capitalist social reproduction from histories of struggle around the commons? As an initial step, we can foreground the importance of naming the violent, differentiated histories that underpin these processes; of avoiding a universalising or romantic view of either the commons or friendship, and instead letting the concepts pull us into the messy, everyday specifics of political struggle, drawing our connections from there, rather than from above. Solidarity, coalition building, accompaniment, mutual association – these all require being honest about what *we don't* have in common as much as what we do.

The poet and activist Harry Josephine Giles, speaking in Glasgow at the Arika festival in November 2024, argued for the importance of acknowledging the differentiated forms that enclosure and dispossession have taken historically. She read from a letter, written in the 'foothills of Beinn Os' in the southern Scottish highlands, in response to Robyn Maynard and Leanne Betasamosake Simpson's book of letters, *Rehearsals for Living*. As Giles outlines:

> In the 18th and 19th centuries the communities who belonged to this forest, this valley, this mountain – and to valleys across the *Gàidhealtachd* – were cleared from their livelihoods, separated from their *dùthchas*, by forceful eviction, managed famine, industrial labour, and, sometimes, when landowners considered it necessary in order to more efficiently replace the people with sheep, fire. They were offered instead the white supremacist promise of settler-colonisation, encouraged or paid or coerced to cross the ocean and steal land, to take a more powerful place in the emerging global order.[38]

The *Fuadach* or 'clearance' is, for Giles, 'a process enabled by and enabling of the settler-colonial project', transforming people into agents of colonial expansion through the settlement of 'frontiers' and by turning them into industrial labourers within the imperial core. As the philosopher Elizabeth A. Povinelli argued in another discussion at that same festival, enclosure across Europe, as violent and brutal as it was, entailed a 'dispossession' *into* 'possessive individualism' – a very different position and level of disposability to the genocidal erasures facing Indigenous and enslaved people at different points in the circuits of colonialism. Acknowledging such difference is vital to any project of solidarity and building common relationality. Simpson and Maynard's beautiful epistolary book, to which Giles is responding, demonstrates the care, criticality and insight required to respond to such histories without flattening difference. Writing from and about their respective positions in Black and Indigenous struggle, their *Rehearsals for Living*, in Katherine McKittrick's words, 'actualizes friendship as correspondence, modeling a mode of togetherness that we can practice, learn from, and revise'.[39] Here we see one way to move beyond the different threads we've analysed in this chapter: the sanitised and corporate notions of 'locality', the imposed ideas of 'universality' and the unhelpful dismissals of particularity.

Letters are key to how *Rehearsals* unfolds, and to many of the examples we have touched upon through this book. Simpson describes the form as such: 'It's messy, It's incomplete. It's gentle. It is, in its simplest form, a record of our relationality'.[40] Through letters, Maynard and Simpson illuminate the kinds of friendship and commoning we see as integral to revolutionary struggle. They do this not by starting from a position of imposed rhetorical commonality, but by illuminating a range of interlinked histories that can help inform contemporary struggle. This requires an approach to temporality that – in resonance with the queer temporalities and 'anti-family trees' we have outlined throughout this book – is in opposition to stagist modes of history that position our current moment as one of singular collapse. As Maynard argues:

> Our respective communities have borne, already, multiple apocalypses that were inflicted upon us, if un-identically, from the 'barbarity time' of genocide/slavery/settler colonialism. The apocalypse is imagined, after all, in most classic Euro-Western settler tropes, in terms of the lack of clean drinking water, the destruction of the places 'we' (they) live, the poisoning of the earth, inhumane and restrictive responses to people left hungry, displaced, in desperation: this is the condition that is already deeply familiar to our kin across Turtle Island and globally.[41]

To look forward, to imagine and start to build new kinds of revolutionary relationality, requires something far harder than bland universalising and proclamations of 'common ground'. It requires modes of communication and spaces of interaction that encourage difference and allow 'friends in common' to emerge in the process.

Friendship is just one tool in this difficult task, and should not constrain how we imagine the future forms that sociality and political belonging might take – both in the struggle against capitalism and after its defeat. As we have argued and attempted to instil throughout this book, any vision of such a future requires reconnecting with history: from 'below', from 'within', and beyond dominant narratives. We can use friendship as a method for building and engaging with history and archives, as well as seeing it as a form *of* archive, helping generate ideas, strategy and revolutionary subjectivities. By connecting such histories to both existing contemporary practices and radical dreams for the future, we illuminate the many ways in which, as we argued at the start of this book, 'the interpersonal is political'. Though it may be uncomfortable for some of us to admit, our friendships are governed, distributed and narrativised in deeply uneven ways, reflecting the wider structures of racial capitalism. By attempting to combine historical and existing perspectives, alongside the 'local-global' perspectives of this final chapter, we can better understand how capitalism co-opts and conditions social life, without assuming this to be complete or totalising. The eras in which friendship was prominent within left-wing struggle – in our analysis, during the late nineteenth century and in the post-1970s 'periodising break' – offer particular insight here, showing not only how the modes of political belonging that predominated in-between these times (the 'comrade', the 'collective worker') need to be reconfigured, but also the productive overlap between many of these ideas.

By considering how friendship can help us think about history, family, work, movement, intergenerational con-nection, the state, and wider forms of solidarity, we've attempted throughout the book to show how friendships' malleability and everyday use makes it important for both revolutionary practice and theory. This feels particularly salient right now, not simply because of the historical arcs we've outlined, but because of the seeming impossibility of the crises that we face. Against the temptation to give up, turn against each other or dictate terms, radical friendship brings us back to the everyday practices that sustain us, whilst also illuminating the systems that will not. To return to E.M. Forster in 1938: 'Personal relationships. Here is something comparatively solid in a world full of violence and cruelty. Not absolutely solid ... We don't know what other people are like. How then can we put any trust in personal relationships, or cling to them in the gathering political storm? In theory we can't. But in practice we can and do.'[42] Forster's insistence that 'in practice we can and do' put our faith in friendship makes clear that part of the power of friendship is that it requires trust and reciprocity – in a world of brutal and isolating regimes, nations and systems, Forster found in friendship something dependable, something open to being made and remade, a forever work-in-progress crafted by those for whom it means something, neither owned nor administered by any one person or group.

As should by now be clear, we don't believe there can be a prescriptive or universal way of thinking about friendship – we don't suggest that friendship is easy, or that it is always good or generative, or that it can solve all our problems. Rather we simply hope we've shown that practices of friendship are political, and that these practices have histories. Under different names and guises, forms of political belonging and ways of galvanising community

have forever preoccupied those interested in transforming how we live. We can easily get bogged down in these
often competing histories, mythologies and definitions
(and we have!), but by gathering these ideas together and
using friendship as an organising principle, we hope to
have shown how we might more usefully draw on the rich
practices of friendship that have happened, are happening
and can happen. Formal and informal, long-lasting and
fleeting, intimate and anonymous, fraught and infuriating
– friendship is central to ways of being in the world, and
to remaking it.

## LETTERTOJEAN (1)

Dear Jean,

Thanks for the note. We've mulled it over, swilled it around and held it up to all the new histories that continue to be made through striving, through irrepressible bonds – the densest bonds! We hope you don't mind being added into our little 'anti-family tree', along with all the other people whose words and ideas we've woven into this book, a 'tissue of relationships' that we hope will extend in unknown ways beyond the pages of this one document.

Perhaps it's harder in this moment to inhabit the density of the relations you describe, let alone the 'literal' nudity (it's cold up here). There is certainly an 'arbitrariness' to all kinds of 'more official, legal, sanctioned, inherited bonds', but you helped us to see that we can make our own lineages, craft our own rituals. Your letter helped us to feel that possibility, to see 'friends in common' and in 'common rhythm' across different points in time and space, to imagine a future where other kinds of relation might emerge, and to try and see where our glimpses of this might lie, in both present and past.

When you spoke of 'love' (and, let's not forget, you put 'love' between quotation marks because it takes so many new and unexpected forms!), you managed, somehow, to conjure a sense of this future – excited, unabashed, in exclamation, probably a little … cringe? But free! – and it felt intimate and political too, whatever that means. It reminded us of times we've turned ourselves 'inside out' through friendship and struggle and the overlap of the two. It made us think of meals shared in draughty community centres covered in strategy maps and post-it notes, of friends-of-friends making it through (the storm, the crossing, the system) and finding a warm bed on the other side, of 'vicarious strength' and fleeting moments of affinity that came just as we were ready to throw in the towel, of the beloved neighbour who gifted us a copy of *Marx and Engels Selected Works* for our 12th birthday (his voice always imprinted in our readings of those biggest of 'ideas') and who was now facing prison for throwing soup at a painting as he approaches his 72nd, of tears and arguments and pints and coffees. Of playing out, going out, coming out. And not just of moments of 'success' (of hands outstretched in prayer as the immigration van doors are opened), but also those of falling out and disagreement and where that took us too.

When you sit alone in a little flat in the Lake District – or in your favourite pub looking out across the River Tyne – trying to finish this book, as wildfires burn and fascism tramples the horizon, and you think about the Japanese warships once built here – the same boats sent to Siberia in an attempt to crush the Bolsheviks after 1917 – and twice a day you hear the wince-inducing whoosh of an RAF F-15 fighter jet flying over Lake Windermere – the same jets that are decimating Gaza, that have rained death on people in Iraq, in Afghanistan, in Syria, in Libya. And the long fog of your battered immune system drifts over your wet eyes, and you think of the friends this system has taken from you and from so many others – and then of that despicable 'doctor' in the airless grey assessment room who said to the dear friend you were accompanying, 'but if you're really struggling in the way you say you are, how can you possibly maintain your friendships in the way you've described'? – and the searing sense that friendship can mean meeting their violence with something equivalent (or at least holding that truth to heart) – and all the 'fuck yous' and 'love yous' you've said and didn't get to say. When you ring them up right then and laugh about a dog and remember that day together and you vibrate gently with the beauty of a life shared – and you know that the nasty, hollow world this system holds on to will never totally eclipse the many other possible worlds, no matter how hard it tries.

When we turn to you and to this letter we can imagine you laughing (hopefully), shrugging (probably), and warning us against that horrible academic impulse to turn everything into a 'concept', an 'idea', a little slice of citable intellectual property, enclosed and privatised. When we turn to things, like friendship, that evade all that, we glimpse beyond the 'idea', so assiduously documented. When we face the 'meat grinder' we don't do it for friendship as captured in any one letter or book, as much as they can (sometimes) help. We start having to figure it out again, in common. As you put it, 'for an "idea", sure. And day to day?'

See you around!

Love from,
Laura & Joel xxx

# *Notes*

## INTRODUCTION: WHY FRIENDSHIP?

1.  Yvonne Blake is the co-founder of Migrants Organising for Rights and Empowerment (MORE), a grassroots, migrant-led organisation in Glasgow campaigning for asylum seekers' and displaced people's access to employment, education, decent housing and dignity. You can find out about MORE via their Facebook page.
2.  The original PDF of this text cited it as being 'From – Jean (1980) Prison de la Santé' and then also 'From "Latitante" – Notes for a movie by Robert Kramer and Félix Guattari Courtesy of Graeme Thomson and Silvia Maglioni'. In 2020 Joel got in contact with Silvia and Graeme who confirmed via email that they had found the letter in the Institut Mémoires de l'édition Contemporaine (IMEC) archives, as part of investigating Félix Guattari and Robert Kramer's 'Latitante Dossier', a collection of documents relating to an unmade Science Fiction film. The letter features in Thompson and Maglioni's wonderful film about this, *In Search of UIQ*.
3.  Foucault, Michel, *Ethics: Subjectivity and Truth*, ed. Paul Rabinow, trans. Robert Hurley and others (New York: The New Press, 1997), p. 136. (The quotation is from an amended version of a 1981 interview in the magazine *Gai Pied* conducted by R. de Ceccaty, J. Danet and J. Le Bitoux, and translated for the collection by John Johnston.)
4.  bell hooks, *Feminist Theory: From Margin to Center* (Boston: South End Press, 1984), p. 71.
5.  Anonymous, 'Friendship as a Form of Life' (2016), p. 4, at http://friendship-as-a-form-of-life.tumblr.com

6. See Aristotle, *The Nicomachean Ethics* (Oxford: Oxford University Press, 2009). Further examples of these long-standing philosophical debates can be found within the Zine, but they are not the focus of this book.

7. Nick Montgomery and clara bergman, *Joyful Militancy: Building Thriving Resistance in Toxic Times* (Chico: AK Press, 2017), p. 58.

8. Anonymous, 'Friendship as a Form of Life', p. 8.

9. Judith Butler, *Precarious Life: The Powers of Mourning and Violence* (London: Verso, 2006), p. 23.

10. Campaign to End Loneliness with Dr Heather McClelland, 'Analysis of Quarterly Report Data Provided by the ONS from the Opinions and Lifestyle Survey for Jan–Dec 2022 Using a Representative Sample of People Aged 16 and Over in Great Britain', and 'The State of Loneliness 2023: ONS Data on Loneliness in Britain' (2023), at https://www.campaigntoendloneliness.org/facts-and-statistics; and https://www.campaigntoendloneliness.org/wp-content/uploads/The-State-of-Loneliness-2023-ONS-data-on-loneliness-in-Britain.pdf

11. Office of the U.S. Surgeon General, *Our Epidemic of Loneliness and Isolation: The U.S. Surgeon General's Advisory on the Healing Effects of Social Connection and Community* (2023), at https://www.hhs.gov/sites/default/files/surgeon-general-social-connection-advisory.pdf.

12. See Daniel Miller and Heather A. Horst, *The Digital and the Human: A Prospectus for Digital Anthropology* (London: Routledge, 2018); Tom Boellstorff, *Coming of Age in Second Life* (Princeton: Princeton University Press, 2008).

13. Robin James interviewed by Chal Ravens and Tom Lea on the No Tags Podcast, at https://notagspodcast.substack.com/p/10-dr-robin-james

14. Bumble for Friends, 'How to Deal with Having No Friends', at https://bumble.com/bff/friendship/no-friends

15. See Adam Smiley Poswolsky, *Friendship in the Age of Loneliness: An Optimist's Guide to Connection* (New York:

Running Press, 2021); Shasta Nelson, *Frientimacy: How to Deepen Friendships for Lifelong Health and Happiness* (New York: Seal Press, 2016); Elizabeth Day, *Friendaholic: Confessions of a Friendship Addict* (London: Fourth Estate, 2023).

16. For a key proponent of 'pleasure activism' see adrienne marie brown, *Pleasure Activism: The Politics of Feeling Good* (London: AK Press, 2019).

17. Hannah Proctor, *Burnout: The Emotional Experience of Political Defeat* (London: Verso, 2024), p. 83.

18. Vincent Bevins, *If We Burn: The Mass Protest Decade and the Missing Revolution* (London: Wildfire, 2023), p. 37.

19. Tori Abernathy, 'We're Here to Make Friends', *Temporary Art Review* (2017), at https://temporaryartreview.com/were-here-to-make-friends

20. For an overview see CrimethInc, *To Change Everything: An Anarchist Appeal* (2018), at https://crimethinc.com/zines/to-change-everything

21. Ruth Kinna, *Anarchism: A Beginners Guide* (Oxford: Oneworld Publications, 2005), p. 130.

22. Bevins, *If We Burn*, p. 259.

23. Endnotes Collective, *Endnotes #4* (2015).

24. Ibid., p. 98.

25. Ibid., p. 85.

26. Ibid., p. 165.

27. Carl Grey Marin and Modhumita Roy, 'Narrative Resistance: A Conversation with Historian Marcus Rediker', *Workplace*, 30 (2018), p. 56.

28. E.g. Isaac Rose, *The Rentier City: Manchester and the Making of the Neoliberal Metropolis.* (London: Repeater, 2024); Proctor, *Burnout*.

29. See Saidiya Hartman, *Wayward Lives, Beautiful Experiments: Intimate Histories of Social Upheaval* (New York: W.W. Norton, 2020); Shola Von Reinhold, *LOTE* (London: Jacaranda Books, 2020).

30. José Esteban Muñoz, *Cruising Utopia: The Then and There of Queer Futurity* (New York: NYU Press, 2009), p. 185.

31. Nicole Wolf, 'Is This Just a Story? Friendships and Fictions for Speculative Alliances: The Yugantar Film Collective (1980–83)', MIRAJ, 7:2 (2018), p. 254.

32. Lola Olufemi, *Experiments in Imagining Otherwise* (London: Verso, 2021), p. 32.

33. David Featherstone, *Resistance, Space and Political Identities: The Making of Counter-Global Networks* (Chichester: Wiley-Blackwell, 2008), p. 12.

## 1   FRIENDS AND FAMILY

1. Stephen Sondheim, 'Being Alive', in *Finishing the Hat: Collected Lyrics with Attendant Comments, Principles, Heresies, Grudges, Whines, and Anecdotes* (London: Virgin Books, 2010), p. 193.

2. Ibid., p. 166.

3. George Zadan, *Sondheim & Co.* (New York: Harper & Row, 1986), p. 124. As an aside, Noah Baumbach's film *Marriage Story* (2019) embraced this less optimistic reading of the song by having Adam Driver's grumpy grown-up theatre kid Charlie sing 'Being Alive' *after* his divorce, as a way to try and explain to his friends how it had felt.

4. Emma Dowling, 'Valorised But Not Valued? Affective Remuneration, Social Reproduction and Feminist Politics Beyond the Recovery', *British Politics*, 11:4 (2016), p. 453.

5. M.E. O'Brien, *Family Abolition: Capitalism and the Communizing of Care* (London: Pluto, 2023), p. 4.

6. Tiffany Lethabo King, 'Black "Feminisms" and Pessimism: Abolishing Moynihan's Negro Family', *Theory and Event*, 21:1 (2018), p. 84.

7. O'Brien, *Family Abolition*, p. 93.

8. See Ruth Wilson Gilmore in conversation with Léopold Lambert, 'Making Abolition Geography in California's Central Valley', *The Funambulist Magazine*, 20 December 2018.

9. O'Brien, *Family Abolition*, p. 53.

10. Ibid., p. 239.
11. Sophie K. Rosa, *Radical Intimacy* (London: Pluto, 2023), p. 167.
12. Ibid., p. 160.
13. Mario Mieli, *Towards a Gay Communism* (London: Pluto, 2018), p. 5.
14. Rosa, *Radical Intimacy*, p. 162.
15. Montgomery and bergman, *Joyful Militancy*, p. 42.
16. Silvia Federici, *Caliban and the Witch: Women, the Body and Primitive Accumulation* (Brooklyn: Autonomedia 2004), p. 63.
17. Cedric Robinson, *Black Marxism: The Making of the Black Radical Tradition* (Chapel Hill: University of North Carolina Press, 1983), p. 26.
18. Gargi Bhattacharyya, *Rethinking Racial Capitalism: Questions of Reproduction and Survival* (Maryland: Rowman & Littlefield International, 2018), p. 5.
19. Emma Dowling, *The Care Crisis: What Caused It and How Can We End It?* (London: Verso, 2021), p. 45.
20. Zoé Samudzi, 'The Master's Tools Will Never Dismantle The Master's House: Abolitionist Feminist Futures' (2020), transcription of the panel discussion at https://silverpress.org/blogs/news/the-master-s-tools-will-never-dismantle-the-master-s-house-abolitionist-feminist-futures
21. Audre Lorde, *A Burst of Light: Essays* (London: Sheba Feminist Publishers, 1988), p. 205.
22. Sara Ahmed, 'Self Care as Warfare' (2019), at https://feministkilljoys.com/2014/08/25/selfcare-as-warfare
23. Lioba Hirsch, *Antiblackness and Global Health: A Response to Ebola in the Colonial Wake* (London: Pluto Press, 2024), p. 92.
24. Bhattacharyya, *Rethinking Racial Capitalism*, p. 44.
25. Dowling, 'Valorised But Not Valued?', p. 454.
26. Julian A. Pitt-Rivers, 'The Paradox of Friendship', *Hau: Journal of Ethnographic Theory*, 6:3 (2016), p. 445.

27. Susan McKinnon and Fenella Cannell (eds.), *Vital Relations: Modernity and the Persistent Life of Kinship* (New Mexico: SAR Press, 2013), p. 3.

28. Janet Carsten, *Cultures of Relatedness: New Approaches to the Study of Kinship* (Cambridge: Cambridge University Press, 2000), p. 5; David M. Schneider, *A Critique of the Study of Kinship* (Ann Arbor: University of Michigan Press, 1984).

29. Kath Weston, *Families We Choose: Gays, Lesbians, and Kinship* (New York: Columbia University Press, 1997).

30. Ibid., p. xiii.

31. Gargi Bhattacharyya writing alongside Nazmia Jamal in *zindabad zine*, 002 (2021), at https://zindabadzine.bigcartel.com

32. Pinko Collective, *After Accountability: A Critical Genealogy of a Concept* (New York: Wendy's Subway, 2023), p. 195.

33. Ibid., p. 194.

34. Sophie Lewis, *Abolish the Family* (London: Verso, 2022), p. 88.

35. Ibid., p. 29.

36. Ibid., p. 86.

37. Ibid., p. 84.

38. Ibid.

39. Ibid., p. 88.

40. Ibid., p. 83.

41. William Morris, *A Dream of John Ball*, at https://www.marxists.org/archive/morris/works/1886/johnball/johnball.htm

42. See William Knight, *Memorials of Thomas Davidson* (Boston: Ginn & Company, 1907), pp. 19–20.

43. Seeds for Change, *Consensus Decision Making: A Short Guide* (2013), at www.seedsforchange.org.uk/shortconsensus

44. L.A. Kauffman, 'The Theology of Consensus', in Astra Taylor and Keith Gessen (eds.), *Occupy! Scenes from Occupied America* (London: Verso, 2011), p. 47.

45. Ibid., p. 49.

46. Sheila Rowbotham, Lynne Segal and Hilary Wainwright, *Beyond the Fragments: Feminism and the Making of Socialism* (Boston: Alyson, 1981), pp. 75–6.

47. Durba Mitra, 'Sisterhood Is X: On Feminist Solidarity Then and Now', *The South Atlantic Quarterly*, 122:3 (2023), p. 434.

48. bell hooks, 'Sisterhood: Political Solidarity Between Women', *Feminist Review*, 23 (1986), p. 127.

49. Mitra, 'Sisterhood Is X', p. 435.

50. hooks, 'Sisterhood', p. 138.

51. Mitra, 'Sisterhood Is X', p. 435.

52. Paul Spicker, *Liberty, Equality, Fraternity* (Bristol: Bristol University Press, 2006), p. 119.

53. Ibid.

54. Peter Kropotkin, *Mutual Aid* (New York: McClure Phillips & Co, 1901), p. 212.

55. Ibid., p. 171.

56. Richard Braithwaite quoted in Marcus Rediker and Peter Linebaugh, *The Many-Headed Hydra: The Hidden History of the Revolutionary Atlantic* (London: Verso, 2012), p. 143.

57. Ibid., p. 206.

58. Jodi Dean, *Comrade* (London: Verso, 2019), p. 52.

59. Ibid., p. 70.

60. Ibid., p. 57.

61. Maria Lind, Michele Masucci and Joanna Warsza (eds.), *Red Love: A Reader on Alexandra Kollontai / Kollontai: A Play by Agneta Pleijel* (London: Sternberg Press, 2019), p. 81.

62. Dean, *Comrade*, p. 57.

63. Ibid., pp. 29–30.

64. Ibid., p. 53.

65. Proctor, *Burnout*, p. 150.

66. Ezra F. Vogel, 'From Friendship to Comradeship: The Change in Personal Relations in Communist China', *The China Quarterly*, 21 (1965).

67. Paul Joscha Kohlenberg, 'The Use of "Comrade" as a Political Instrument in the Chinese Communist Party, from Mao to Xi', *The China Quarterly*, 77 (2017), p. 73.

68. Ibid., p. 91.
69. See ibid., pp. 88, 94.
70. Dean, *Comrade*, p. 22.
71. Jane McAlevey, *No Shortcuts: Organizing for Power in the New Gilded Age* (New York: Oxford University Press, 2017), p. 209.
72. Dean, *Comrade*, p. 35.
73. Ibid., p. 64.
74. Alexandra Kollontai, 'Make Way for Winged Eros: A Letter to Working Youth', in *Selected Writings* (London: Allison & Busby, 1977), p. 291.
75. Ibid., p. 285.
76. Nazan Üstündağ, *The Mother, the Politician, and the Guerrilla: Women's Political Imagination in the Kurdish Movement* (New York: Fordham University Press, 2023), p. 142.
77. Interview with Nazan Üstündağ at www.jadaliyya.com/Details/45907
78. Üstündağ, *The Mother, the Politician, and the Guerrilla*, p. 142.
79. Ibid.
80. Ibid., p. 143.
81. David Webb, 'On Friendship: Derrida, Foucault, and the Practice of Becoming', *Research in Phenomenology*, 33:1 (2002), pp. 119–40.
82. Elif Sarican and Dilar Dirik, 'Hevaltî – Revolutionary Friendship as Radical Care', *Performing Borders e-journal*, 2 (2022), 'Rallying the Commons', at https://performingborders.live/ejournal/hevalti-revolutionary-friendship-as-radical-care
83. Ibid.
84. Leela Gandhi, *Affective Communities* (Durham, NC: Duke University Press, 2006), p. 184.
85. Kollontai, 'Make Way for Winged Eros', p. 291.

## 2   WORK FRIENDS

1. Nielson, 'Tops of 2020: Nielsen Streaming Unwrapped', at www.nielsen.com/insights/2021/tops-of-2020-nielsen-streaming-unwrapped

2. See Kate Williams, 'Billie Eilish Wants to Show You Her Room', *Elle*, 29 March 2019, at www.elle.com/culture/music/a26984783/billie-eilish-when-we-all-fall-asleep

3. Jason Okundaye, 'The Blair Show', *Tribune*, 29 June 2020, at https://tribunemag.co.uk/2020/06/the-blair-show-tv

4. See James Moules, 'Starmer Vows "Sweeping Changes" to Tackle "Bulging Benefits Bill"', Labour List, 24 November 2024, at https://labourlist.org/2024/11/labour-keir-starmer-benefits-reform-liz-kendall

5. Bhattacharyya, *Rethinking Racial Capitalism*, p. 42.

6. Malcolm Chase, *Early Trade Unionism: Fraternity, Skill and the Politics of Labour* (Aldershot: Ashgate, 2000), p. 4.

7. Quoted in Owen Jones, 'Class War: Thatcher's Attack on Trade Unions, Industry and Working-class Identity', Verso blog, 8 April 2013, at www.versobooks.com/en-gb/blogs/news/1274-class-war-thatcher-s-attack-on-trade-unions-industry-and-working-class-identity

8. Kornel Chang, 'Circulating Race and Empire: Transnational Labor Activism and the Politics of Anti-Asian Agitation in the Anglo-American Pacific World, 1880–1910', *Journal of American History*, 96 (2009), p. 685.

9. Ibid.

10. Mae M. Ngai, 'Chinese Gold Miners and the "Chinese Question" in Nineteenth-Century California and Victoria', *The Journal of American History*, 101 (2015), p. 1103.

11. Gavin Mueller, *Breaking Things at Work: The Luddites Are Right About Why You Hate Your Job* (London: Verso, 2021), p. 20.

12. Katrina Navickas, 'The Search for "General Ludd": The Mythology of Luddism', *Social History*, 30 (2005), p. 291.

13. Ibid.

14. Ibid., p. 293.

15. Ibid.

16. See Seerut K. Chawla, at https://x.com/seerutkchawla/status/1397559056991203332

17. Dive into the full thread (if you dare) at www.metafilter.com/151267/Wheres-My-Cut-On-Unpaid-Emotional-Labor

18. Jess Zimmerman, '"Where's My Cut?": On Unpaid Emotional Labor', The Toast, 13 July 2015, at https://the-toast.net/2015/07/13/emotional-labor/2

19. Ibid.

20. Hazel Cills, 'The Overuse of "Emotional Labor" Turns All Relationships Into Work', Jezebel, 20 November 2019, at www.jezebel.com/the-overuse-of-emotional-labor-turns-all-relationships-1839958498

21. Arlie Hochschild interviewed by Julie Beck, 'The Concept Creep of "Emotional Labor"', The Atlantic, 26 November 2018, at www.theatlantic.com/family/archive/2018/11/arlie-hochschild-housework-isnt-emotional-labor/576637

22. Gemma Hartley, Fed Up: Emotional Labor, Women, and the Way Forward (San Francisco: HarperOne, 2018).

23. Sheryl Sandberg, Lean In: Women, Work, and the Will to Lead (London: W.H. Allen, 2013), For a (far more useful) critique of this tendency, see Dawn Foster, Lean Out (London: Repeater, 2016); Kim Hong Nguyen, Mean Girl Feminism: How White Feminists Gaslight, Gatekeep, and Girlboss (Illinois: University of Illinois Press, 2024).

24. Lola Olufemi, Feminism, Interrupted: Disrupting Power (London, Pluto: 2020), p. 4.

25. Arlie Hochschild, The Managed Heart: Commercialization of Human Feeling (Berkeley: University of California Press, 1983).

26. Ibid., p. 7.

27. Ibid., p. 198.

28. Ibid., p. 33.

29. Ibid., p. 7.

30. Paul Brook, 'In Critical Defence of "Emotional Labour": Refuting Bolton's Critique of Hochschild's Concept', Work Employment and Society, 23:3 (2009), p. 8.

31. See Louise Toupin, *Wages for Housework: A History of an International Feminist Movement, 1972–77* (London: Pluto, 2018).

32. Hochschild and Beck, 'The Concept Creep of "Emotional Labor"'.

33. Marie Heřmanová, 'HandsOn Screen: Influencers and Digital Intimacy on Instagram', Cultural Anthropology blog, 1 December 2022, at https://culanth.org/fieldsights/handson-screen-influencers-and-digital-intimacy-on-instagram

34. See Dominic Rushe, 'WhatsApp: Facebook Acquires Messaging Service in $19bn Deal', *The Guardian*, 20 February 2014, at www.theguardian.com/technology/2014/feb/19/facebook-buys-whatsapp-16bn-deal

35. Zuckerberg interviewed by Mike Isaac, 'Mark Zuckerberg Taps the Strengths of WhatsApp', *New York Times*, 8 November 2013, at www.nytimes.com/2023/11/08/technology/mark-zuckerberg-whatsapp.html

36. See Tom Wall, 'Facebook Office Cleaner Who Led Protests at London Site Fears for His Job', *The Guardian*, 12 September 2021, at www.theguardian.com/technology/2021/sep/12/facebook-office-cleaner-who-led-protests-at-london-site-fears-for-his-job

37. Peter Elkind, Jack Gillum and Craig Silverman, 'How Facebook Undermines Privacy Protections for Its 2 Billion WhatsApp Users', ProPublica, 7 September 2021, at www.propublica.org/article/how-facebook-undermines-privacy-protections-for-its-2-billion-whatsapp-users

38. Brook, 'In Critical Defence of "Emotional Labour"', p. 13.

39. See Juno Mac and Molly Smith, *Revolting Prostitutes: The Fight for Sex Workers' Rights* (London: Verso, 2018).

40. Prole, *Abolish Restaurants: A Worker's Critique of the Food Service Industry* (Oakland: PM Press, Pamphlet Series No. 0005 / prole.info, 2010).

41. Anahit Behrooz, *BFFs: The Radical Potential of Female Friendship* (404 Ink Limited, 2023), pp. 71–2. As Behrooz

goes on to explain, the 'brunch friend' idea is inspired by a conversation in Noah Baumbach and Greta Gerwig's 2012 film *Frances Ha*.

42. See Terry Nguyen, 'How Brunch Became Political', Vox, 18 November 2020, at www.vox.com/the-goods/21572182/brunch-biden-political-indifference

## CONVERSATION WITH GRACIE MAE BRADLEY

1. Gracie Mae Bradley, 'On Hospitality', 23 June 2023, at https://inrelativeopacity.substack.com/p/on-hospitality
2. See Neske Baerwaldt and Wiebe Ruijtenberg, De Verbranders, at https://soundcloud.com/de-verbranders

## 3   FRIENDS OF FRIENDS

1. Bradley, 'On Hospitality'.
2. Letter from George Thompson to William Lloyd Garrison (1837), cited in Ronald M. Gifford 'George Thompson and Transatlantic Anti-Slavery, 1831–1865', PhD thesis, Indiana University, 1999, p. 186.
3. See Eric Hobsbawm, 'The Tramping Artisan', *Economic History Review*, 3 (1951), pp. 299–320.
4. Constance Bantman, *The French Anarchists in London, 1880–1914: Exile and Transnationalism in the First Globalisation* (Liverpool: Liverpool University Press, 2013), p. 8.
5. Annie Besant, *An Autobiography* (Madras: The Theosophical Publishing House, 1939), p. 292–3.
6. E. Lees to R. MacDonald, 21 April 1892, 84–6, 30/69, MacDonald Papers. PRO.
7. 'Comrade A. Henry's Tour in the North' (letter from Agnes Henry to *Freedom*, 13 October 1893), at https://forgottenanarchism.wordpress.com/category/agnes-henry
8. O'Connor wrote: 'All the links were now perfect. London, Newcastle, Carlisle, Edinburgh and Glasgow had now become forged as it were together.' NS, 21 July 1838, cited

in Humphrey Southall, 'Agitate! Agitate! Organize! Political Travellers and the Construction of a National Politics, 1839–1880', *Transactions of the Institute of British Geographers*, 21:1 (1996), p. 181.

9. 'Comrade A. Henry's Tour in the North' (letter from Agnes Henry to *Freedom*).

10. Ole Birk Laursen, 'Anti-Colonialism, Terrorism and the "Politics of Friendship": Virendranath Chattopadhyaya and the European Anarchist Movement, 1910–1927', *Anarchist Studies*, 27 (2019), p. 58.

11. Nadine Willem, 'Transnational Anarchism, Japanese Revolutionary Connections, and the Personal Politics of Exile', *The Historical Journal*, 61 (2018), p. 720.

12. George R. Taylor, *Leaders of Socialism, Past and Present* (London, 1910), p. 119.

13. David Prynn, 'The Clarion Clubs, Rambling and the Holiday Associations in Britain since the 1890s', *Journal of Contemporary History*, 11 (1976), pp. 65–77.

14. *The Clarion*, 29 February 1896.

15. 'With the "Clarion" Van', *Evening Telegraph* (Dundee, Scotland), 13 September 1900, p. 4.

16. For discussion of the characterisation of British socialism as very much distinct from socialism on the continent, see Duncan Tanner, 'The Development of British Socialism, 1900–1918', *Parliamentary History*, 16:1 (1997), pp. 48–66.

17. Leela Gandhi, *Affective Communities*, p. 10.

18. Jennifer Mason, *Affinities: Potent Connections in Personal Life* (Cambridge: Polity, 2018), p. 186.

19. Ibid., p. 2.

20. Mireille Rosello, *Postcolonial Hospitality: The Immigrant as Guest* (Stanford: Stanford University Press, 2001), p. 176.

21. Ole Birk Laursen examines this in reference to Indian Anarchists in Europe in the early twentieth century. See Laursen, 'Anti-Colonialism, Terrorism and the "Politics of Friendship"'.

22. See *Rum Lad* by Steve Larder, at www.stevelarder.co.uk/index.php/rumladzine; Isy Morgenmuffel, *Diary of a Miscreant: A Morgenmuffel Zine Anthology* (London: Last Hours, 2009); Crimethinc, at https://crimethinc.com

23. The Schnews archives is available at https://schnews.org

24. See Peter Gelderloos, *How Nonviolence Protects the State* (Oakland: PM Press, 2007); Dysophia, *What About the Rapists? Anarchist Approaches to Crime and Justice* (Bristol: Active Distribution, 2014/2021).

25. The piece is available online in various places, including the Anarchist Library: https://theanarchistlibrary.org/library/andrew-x-give-up-activism

26. Indigenous Action, *Accomplices Not Allies: An Indigenous Perspective* (2014), at www.indigenousaction.org/accomplices-not-allies-abolishing-the-ally-industrial-complex

27. Available online and in C.B. Daring, J. Rogue, Deric Shannon and Abbey Volcano (eds.), *Queering Anarchism: Addressing and Undressing Power and Desire* (Oakland: AK Press, 2012).

28. Lee P, *Pals. The Radical Possibilities of Friendship* (2023). Self-published zine, at www.mespantsdequeer.com/livres-neufs-/p/pals-the-radical-possibilities-of-friendship

29. *Radical Transfeminism* is not available online, but there is a copy at Glasgow Women's Library, and Nat Raha's ongoing work includes her recent book with Mijke van der Drift, *Trans Femme Futures: Abolitionist Ethics for Transfeminist Worlds* (London: Pluto, 2024). *Fucking Trans Women* can be bought at http://fuckingtranswomen.org, with funds going to Mira Bellwether's family, since the sad news of her passing in 2022.

## 4  OLD FRIENDS

1. Alex Wheatle, 'I Felt So Alone and Rejected – Until My Prison Cellmate Taught Me About Belonging', *The Guardian*, 29 December 2021, at www.theguardian.com/

lifeandstyle/2021/dec/29/i-felt-so-alone-and-rejected-until-my-prison-cellmate-taught-me-about-belonging

2. Stuart Hall, 'Life and Times of the First New Left', *New Left Review*, 61 (2010), at https://newleftreview.org/issues/ii61/articles/stuart-hall-life-and-times-of-the-first-new-left

3. Proctor, *Burnout*, p. 20.

4. Sally Weale, 'Britain Is One of World's Most Age-segregated Countries, Study Finds', *The Guardian*, 7 January 2020, at www.theguardian.com/society/2020/jan/07/britain-age-segregated-countries-world-age-apartheid

5. Penelope Lively, *Moon Tiger* (New York: Grove Press, 1988), p. 2.

6. Ben Walters reviewing *All of Us Strangers* – another film heavy with themes of intergenerational love and trauma. See Walters, 'All of Us Strangers: Andrew Haigh's Glorious Magic-Realist Meditation on Grief', BFI, 23 January 2024, at www.bfi.org.uk/sight-and-sound/reviews/all-us-strangers-andrew-haighs-glorious-magic-realist-meditation-grief#

7. Lynne Segal, *Out of Time: The Pleasures and Perils of Ageing* (London: Verso, 2013), p. 260.

8. 'Towards the Horizon of Abolition: A Conversation with Mariame Kaba', The Next System Project, 9 November 2017, at https://thenextsystem.org/learn/stories/towards-horizon-abolition-conversation-mariame-kaba

9. Ajamu X, Interview by E-J Scott, 8 May 2020, at https://wyqs.co.uk/stories/ajamu-x-for-the-record/full-interview

10. Ajamu X, E-J Scott and Laura Forster, 'Queer Lives: Public History and the Queer Archive', History Workshop Online, at www.historyworkshop.org.uk/podcast/queer-lives-public-history-and-the-queer-archive

11. Stuart Hall, 'Constituting an Archive', *Third Text*, 15:54 (2001), p. 89.

12. Ann Cvetkovich, *An Archive of Feelings: Trauma, Sexuality and Lesbian Public Cultures* (Durham, NC: Duke University Press, 2003) p. 242.

13. Lynne Segal, *Making Trouble: Life and Politics* (London: Verso, 2007), p. 173.

14. Alan Bray, *The Friend* (Chicago: University of Chicago Press, 2003), p. 5.

15. See https://lesbianherstoryarchives.org/about

16. David Scott, *Stuart Hall's Voice: Intimations of an Ethics of Receptive Generosity* (Durham, NC: Duke University Press, 2017).

17. Ibid.

18. Ibid., pp. 7–8.

19. Sarah Schulman, *Conflict Is Not Abuse: Overstating Harm, Community Responsibility, and the Duty of Repair* (Vancouver: Arsenal Pulp Press, 2016), p. 135.

20. Amanda Herbert, 'Queer Intimacy: Speaking with the Dead in Eighteenth-Century Britain', *Gender and History*, 31:1 (2019), pp. 32–3.

21. Ibid., p. 25.

22. Ibid., p. 33.

23. W. Scott Haine, '"Café Friend": Friendship and Fraternity in Parisian Working-Class Cafés, 1850–1914', *Journal of Contemporary History*, 27:4 (1992), p. 607.

24. Ibid., p. 622.

25. Ibid., p. 607.

26. Ibid., pp. 615–16.

27. Ibid., p. 616.

28. Ibid., p. 618.

29. Martin Phillip Johnson, *The Paradise of Association: Political Culture and Popular Organisations in the Paris Commune of 1871* (Ann Arbor: University of Michigan Press, 1996), p. 19.

30. *The Bee Hive*, 24 June 1871.

31. Scott Haine, '"Café Friend"', pp. 619–20.

32. Nazan Üstündağ, *The Mother, the Politician, and the Guerrilla: Women's Political Imagination in the Kurdish Movement* (New York: Fordham University Press, 2023), p. 131.

33. Ibid., p. 143.

34. Ibid., p. 131.

35. Debbie Bookchin, Emre Şahin and Marina Sitrin, 'Eyewit-nesses to the Rojava Revolution: Hevaltî and Dignity', *ROAR Magazine*, 22 November 2019, at https://roarmag.org/essays/eyewitnesses-to-the-rojava-revolution-hevalti-and-dignity

36. Ibid.

37. Üstündağ, *The Mother, the Politician, and the Guerrilla*, p. 149.

38. Ibid., p. 142.

39. Harry Waveney, 'Resistance is Life: Hevaltî, Çay and Auld Lang Syne', at www.planetmagazine.org.uk/planet-extra/resistance-life

40. Ibid.

41. Segal, *Out of Time*, p. 223.

## CONVERSATION WITH LUKE DE NORONHA

1. For Paul Gilroy's discussion of the concept of convivial-ity see his *After Empire: Melancholia or Convivial Culture?* (London: Routledge, 2004); see also Luke de Noronha, 'The Conviviality of the Overpoliced, Detained and Expelled: Refusing Race and Salvaging the Human at the Borders of Britain', *Sociological Review*, 70 (2022).

## 5   BAD FRIENDS

1. Walter Benjamin, *The Arcades Project*, trans. Howard Eiland and Kevin McLaughlin (Cambridge, MA: Harvard University Press, 1999), p. 13.

2. See Anna Minton, *Ground Control: Fear and Happi-ness in the Twenty-First-Century City* (London: Penguin, 2009); and Anna Minton, *Big Capital: Who Is London For?* (London: Penguin, 2017).

3. Rafael Behr, 'They Sold Our Streets and Nobody Noticed', *The Guardian*, 5 July 2009, at www.theguardian.com/books/2009/jul/05/ground-control-anna-minton-review

4. Minton, *Ground Control*, p. 143.

5. Cara Chellew, 'Accessibility Measure or Exclusive Architecture?', *Azure Magazine*, 29 July 2020, at www.azuremagazine.com/article/accessibility-measure-or-exclusive-architecture

6. Krista, 'Anti-Homeless Measures Are Anti-Sitting Disability', My Upright Life, 8 July 2021, at https://myuprightlife.com/index.php/2021/07/08/anti-homeless-measures-are-anti-sitting-disability

7. Alex Vitale, *The End of Policing* (London: Verso, 2017), p. 176.

8. Arun Kundnani interviewed by Jordan T. Camp and Christina Heatherton, 'Total Policing and the Global Surveillance Empire Today: An Interview with Arun Kundnani', in *Policing the Planet: Why the Policing Crisis Led to Black Lives Matter* (London: Verso, 2016), p. 75.

9. Ibid.

10. O'Brien, *Family Abolition*, p. 71.

11. Luke de Noronha, 'Gangs Policing, Deportation, and the Criminalisation of Friendship', History Workshop Online, 8 July 2020, at www.historyworkshop.org.uk/black-history/gangs-policing-deportation-and-the-criminalisation-of-friendship

12. Ibid.

13. Ibid.

14. Nana Varveropoulou, 'No Man's Land', at www.nanav.com/no-man-s-land

15. Brighton Photo Biennial 2018 Showcase: Nana Varveropoulou, at https://photoworks.org.uk/brighton-photo-biennial-2018-showcase-nana-varveropoulou/#page-gallery-11

16. Anna Maguire, 'Hostile Environments: Refugees, Asylum Seekers and the Politics of Loneliness', *new formations*, 109 (2023), p. 49.

17. Cathy J. Cohen, 'Punks, Bulldaggers, and Welfare Queens: The Radical Potential of Queer Politics?', *GLQ: A Journal of Lesbian and Gay Studies*, 3 (1997), pp. 437–65.

18. De Noronha, 'Gangs Policing, Deportation, and the Criminalisation of Friendship'.
19. John Quail, *The Slow Burning Fuse: The Lost History of the British Anarchists* (London: Paladin, 1978), p. 109.
20. Bantman, *French Anarchists in London*, pp. 90–1.
21. D.J. Nicholl, 'The Walsall Anarchists', *The Journal of the Vigilance Association for the Defence of Personal Rights*, 171 (15 November 1896), p. 80.
22. G.K. Chesterton, *The Man Who Was Thursday: A Nightmare* (1908); Joseph Conrad, *The Secret Agent* (1907).
23. 'The Late Commune: The Refugees in London Scenes', reprinted from the *London Echo* in *The New York Times*, 23 September 1871.
24. Adolphe Smith, 'Political Refugees', in Walter Besant, *London in the Nineteenth Century* (London, 1909), p. 401.
25. John C. Raines speaking in *1971*, dir. Johanna Hamilton, First Run Features, 2014.
26. Nathan Stephens Griffin, '"Everyone Was Questioning Everything": Understanding the Derailing Impact of Undercover Policing on the Lives of UK Environmentalists', *Social Movement Studies*, 20 (2021), pp. 459–77.
27. Tom Foot, 'Secret Mission! How Detective Grew a Beard and Started to Wear Corduroy to Infiltrate Activist Groups', *Camden New Journal*, 19 November 2020, at www.camdennewjournal.co.uk/article/secret-mission-how-detective-grew-a-beard-and-started-to-wear-corduroy-to-infiltrate-activist-groups
28. Peter Francis quoted as 'Peter Black' in Rob Evans and Paul Lewis, *Undercover: The True Story of Britain's Secret Police* (London: Faber, 2013), p. 131.
29. The (redacted) SDS Tradecraft Manual is available via the Undercover Policing Inquiry at www.ucpi.org.uk/publications/sds-tradecraft-manual
30. Foot, 'Secret Mission!'
31. 'Gist of T1 witness statements received by the UCPI from the following officers who have real and cover name restric-

tion – HN21, HN41, HN109, HN241, HN302, HN341, HN355.1', ref: UCPI0000034307, publication date: 21 Apr 2021, at www.ucpi.org.uk/publications/gist-of-t1-witness-statements-real-and-cover-name-restriction

32. 'Naomi', in *Deep Deception: The Story of the Spycop Network, By the Women Who Uncovered the Shocking Truth* (London: Penguin/Ebury Press, 2022), p. 265.

33. Tom Fowler interviewed by Brace Beldon and Liz Franczak on the TrueAnon Podcast, 17 December 2020, Episode 122: Spycops Undercover, at www.patreon.com/posts/episode-122-44747020

34. Verity Smith interviewed by Tom Anderson in Corporate Watch/Rebecca Fisher (ed.), *Managing Democracy: Managing Dissent* (London: Freedom Press, 2013), p. 278.

35. SDS Tradecraft Manual, p. 27.

36. Fowler on TrueAnon Podcast.

37. Ibid.

38. 'Alison', in *Deep Deception*, p. 264.

39. Fowler on TrueAnon Podcast.

40. Ibid.

41. 'Alison', in *Deep Deception*, p. 265.

42. SDS Tradecraft Binder 2, Appendix D, pp. 67, 68, 69, at www.ucpi.org.uk/wp-content/uploads/2018/03/20180319-TC-Documents_Final_Version.pdf

43. See Damien Gayle, 'Five Just Stop Oil Activists Receive Record Sentences For Planning to Block M25', *The Guardian*, 18 July 2024, at www.theguardian.com/environment/article/2024/jul/18/five-just-stop-oil-supporters-jailed-over-protest-that-blocked-m25

44. See Rob Evans, '1,200 Undercover Police Officers Operating Across England and Wales', *The Guardian*, 14 October 2014, at www.theguardian.com/uk-news/2014/oct/14/police-1200-undercover-officers-hmic-covert-family-stephen-lawrence. To be clear, this figure includes what the police would frame as 'non-political' undercover policing too.

45. Sita Balani, 'Infiltrating the Family', Public Books, 7 February 2024, at www.publicbooks.org/infiltrating-the-family
46. 'Lisa', in *Deep Deception*, p. 187.

## 6    FRIENDS IN COMMON

1.  Tim Irwin, *We Jam Econo: The Story of the Minutemen*, Rocket Fuel Films Productions, 2005.
2.  Stewart Smith, 'I Live Sweat But I Dream Light Years: Minutemen's Double Nickels On The Dime at 40', The Quietus, 3 July 2024, at https://thequietus.com/opinion-and-essays/anniversary/the-minutemen-double-nickels-on-the-dime-review
3.  David A. Banks, *The City Authentic: How the Attention Economy Builds Urban America* (Berkeley: University of California Press), pp. 9–10.
4.  Huey P. Newton, 'The Women's Liberation and Gay Liberation Movements' (1970), at www.blackpast.org/african-american-history/speeches-african-american-history/huey-p-newton-women-s-liberation-and-gay-liberation-movements
5.  M.E. O'Brien thread available at: https://bsky.app/profile/genderhorizon.com/post/3lewknwzcoc2w
6.  Olufemi, *Feminism, Interrupted*, p. 120.
7.  Jeremy Gilbert, 'Notes Towards a Theory of Solidarity (talk from the Goldsmiths teach-out)', at https://jeremygilbertwriting.wordpress.com/2018/05/01/notes-towards-a-theory-of-solidarity-talk-from-the-goldsmiths-teach-out
8.  Denise Riley, *The Words of Selves: Identification, Solidarity, Irony* (Stanford: Stanford University Press, 2000), p. 174.
9.  Ibid., p. 177.
10. Ibid., p. 181.
11. Olufemi, *Feminism, Interrupted*, p. 120.
12. Harry Blatterer, 'Friendship and Solidarity', *European Journal of Social Theory*, 25 (2022), p. 229.

13. Ibid.
14. Ibid.
15. Alecia Simmonds, 'Friendship, Imperial Violence and the Law of Nations: The Case of Late-Eighteenth Century British Oceania', *Journal of Imperial and Commonwealth History*, 42:4 (2014), pp. 660–1.
16. Rosalind Carr, 'Politeness, Civility, and Violence on the New South Wales "Frontier," 1788–1816', *Journal of British Studies*, 62:1 (2023), pp. 21–48.
17. Simmonds, 'Friendship, Imperial Violence and the Law of Nations', p. 651.
18. Carr, 'Politeness, Civility, and Violence', p. 47.
19. Ibid., p. 43.
20. E.M. Forster, 'What I Believe', *The Nation*, 16 July 1938.
21. Ibid.
22. Ibid.
23. David Harvey, *Spaces of Hope* (Berkeley: University of California Press, 2000), p. 55.
24. Rose, *The Rentier City*, p. 160–1.
25. Michael Hardt and Antonio Negri, *Empire* (Cambridge, MA: Harvard University Press, 2001), p. 45.
26. Katrina Navickas, *Protest and the Politics of Space and Place, 1789–1848* (Manchester: Manchester University Press, 2017), pp. 18–19.
27. Doreen Massey, 'Landscape/Space/Politics: An Essay', at https://thefutureoflandscape.wordpress.com/landscapespacepolitics-an-essay
28. Doreen Massey, 'Places and Their Pasts', *History Workshop Journal*, 39 (1995), p. 183.
29. Paul Gilroy, *The Black Atlantic: Modernity and Double Consciousness* (London: Verso, 1993), pp. 16–17; James Clifford, 'Travelling Cultures', in Lawrence Grossberg et al. (eds.) *Cultural Studies* (New York: Routledge, 1992).
30. Kirkpatrick Sale, *Rebels Against the Future: The Luddites and Their War on the Industrial Revolution: Lessons for the*

*Computer Age* (San Francisco: Addison-Welsley, 1995), p. 275.

31. Ibid., p. 277.

32. David Featherstone, 'Towards the Relational Construction of Militant Particularisms: Or Why the Geographies of Past Struggles Matter for Resistance to Neoliberal Globalisation', *Antipode*, 37 (2005), p. 251.

33. Massey, 'Landscape/Space/Politics'.

34. Priyamvada Gopal, *Insurgent Empire: Anticolonial Resistance and British Dissent* (London: Verso, 2019), pp. 10–11.

35. David Featherstone, *Solidarity: Hidden Histories and Geographies of Internationalism* (London: Bloomsbury, 2012), p. 4.

36. Massey, 'Landscape/Space/Politics'.

37. Miriam Ticktin, 'Building a Feminist Commons in the Time of Covid-19', *Signs: Journal of Women and Culture in Society* symposium, 'Feminists Theorize Covid-19', October 2020, at http://signsjournal.org/covid/ticktin

38. Harry Josephine Giles, 'Rehearsals for Living' Response. Written, offered and read by Harry Josephine Giles at the Rehearsals for Living event at Arika's Episode 11: To End the World As We Know It, on 16 November 2024 at Tramway, Glasgow. Full text at https://arika.org.uk/rehearsals-for-living

39. Katherine McKittrick, inside cover review of Robyn Maynard and Leanne Betasamosake Simpson, *Rehearsals for Living* (Chicago: Haymarket Books, 2022).

40. Maynard and Simpson, *Rehearsals for Living*, p. 34.

41. Ibid., p. 9.

42. Forster, 'What I Believe'.

## The Pluto Press Newsletter

Hello friend of Pluto!

Want to stay on top of the best radical books
we publish?

Then sign up to be the first to hear about our
new books, as well as special events,
podcasts and videos.

You'll also get 50% off your first order with us
when you sign up.

Come and join us!

Go to bit.ly/PlutoNewsletter